HUMBER CARS
THE POST-WAR YEARS

STEPHEN LEWIS

AMBERLEY

Above: Princess Elizabeth inspects a new Mk1 Humber Super Snipe at the War Memorial Park in Coventry on 22 May 1948. This special event was held to show the resurgence of industry based in Coventry and the rebuilding of the city centre following the devastation suffered during the Second World War. (Leon Gibbs)

Front cover: The front cover of the 1962 Series 4 Super Snipe brochure, featuring an illustration painted by the renowned commercial artist Frank Wootton. The illustration was designed to convey a slight mystical 'Shangri-La' image, which sets the car up nicely. Frank had a commission from Rootes for numerous brochure pictures during the 1950s and 60s before moving on to work for BOAC, create aviation pictures for the RAF and equine subjects. He died in 1998 aged eighty-three.

Rear cover: Taken in 1985 with the author on the right with his late father Donald, showing two early purchases of Humbers that this book covers. On the left, a 1958 Series 1 Hawk, found abandoned by a parking meter in Kingston upon Thames and restored. On the right, a 1954 Mark 6A Hawk purchased in Worcester in original condition. (South London Press)

First published 2021

Amberley Publishing
The Hill, Stroud, Gloucestershire, GL5 4EP
www.amberley-books.com

Copyright © Stephen Lewis, 2021

The right of Stephen Lewis to be identified as the Author of this work has been asserted in accordance with the Copyrights, Designs and Patents Act 1988.

ISBN: 978 1 4456 9758 1 (print)
ISBN: 978 1 4456 9759 8 (ebook)

British Library Cataloguing in Publication Data. A catalogue record for this book is available from the British Library.

Typeset in 10pt on 13pt Celeste.
Typesetting by SJmagic DESIGN SERVICES, India.
Printed in the UK.

Contents

Introduction

The name Humber derives from Thomas Humber, born in Sheffield in 1841, who made his name manufacturing bicycles during the late 1890s. Thomas Humber retired but the expanding company progressed to the fitting of a petrol engine to a three-wheeled vehicle in 1899, the Humber Motor Sociable, thereby making Great Britain one of the first countries in the world to build a motor car. He progressed by expanding the company to factories in Beeston in Nottinghamshire and finally to Coventry.

Motor car production in general evolved in the early part of the twentieth century, with Humber rapidly gaining a reputation for quality and value for money until financial difficulties affected the company in the late 1920s.

William and Reginald Rootes, two brothers from Hawkhurst in Kent, followed their father, also William, into the burgeoning motor car sales and repair business. William Junior had been apprenticed to the Singer Motor Company at sixteen years of age at their factory in Coventry. It's strange to think that years later, in 1956, he and his brother Reginald would take over Singer. Reginald had taken a more academic route and ended up joining the Admiralty. 1914 saw the start of the First World War and both brothers joined the services; Billy joined the Royal Navy Reserve as a Lieutenant and Reggie, the Civil Service.

Following the First World War, as he had been involved in companies that rebuilt aero engines, Billy decided that he, his brother and his father should start their own business. In 1917 Rootes Ltd became an entity, initially repairing aircraft engines but then distributing,

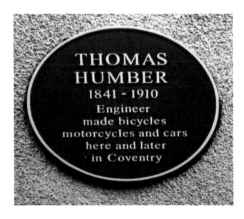

The Thomas Humber wall plaque on the old Beeston, Nottingham, Humber factory. (Ray Sellers)

selling and servicing cars. New facilities were taken in Maidstone in Kent and the business expanded. They were now looking at the production of motor cars. Hillman and then Humber were companies seeking financial support to stay solvent, creating an opportunity as they took a controlling interest in Hillman in 1927 and Humber in 1928. These acquisitions were the start of what was to become the Rootes Group empire, which would eventually acquire Sunbeam and Singer and the commercial vehicle companies Commer and Karrier.

Building on Humber's reputation for quality, models such as the Snipe, Super Snipe, Imperial and Pullman entered the market to compete in the UK with Rover, Daimler, Bentley and Rolls-Royce.

The start of the Second World War in 1939 meant a change to production of munitions, military vehicles and aircraft with the building of new 'shadow' factories to undertake this extensive work.

This book looks at how Humber were able to reassert themselves in the post-war years, continuing the development of the pre-war models and new designs.

With stricter financial controls to arrest losses in the late 1950s, a change to more economical Humber motoring came with the introduction of the Sceptre model in 1963, which was aimed at a younger customer base. 'Badge engineering' was introduced throughout the Rootes Group range in order to reduce costs while maintaining market position. Alas, it was not enough.

The story concludes with the emergence of Chrysler of the USA and their wish to establish a foothold in the UK vehicle market. Their takeover of the Rootes Group in 1967 saw a gradual wind-down of the individual Rootes divisions. In 1976, the last Sceptre rolled off the production line, bringing to an end 'Humber' as a marque.

In the present-day classic car world, Humber has not been deemed desirable and prices compared to other makes has been low. However, the marque is now attracting the interest it deserves. This is aided by the availability of new parts and technical advice through the club that caters for these cars, the Post Vintage Humber Car Club (referred to as the 'Club' throughout the book). The Club is a member of the Association of Rootes Car Clubs and has access to a major resource of original Rootes factory drawings and technical data available through the Rootes Archive Centre Trust.

As well as the Post Vintage Humber Car Club, which has members throughout the UK and around the world, other Humber and Rootes clubs exist in territories where Humbers were exported.

The archetypal picture of the Rootes brothers, with Sir Reginald on the left and Lord William Rootes on the right. The picture shows them at the height of the Rootes Group empire. (Rootes Archive Centre Trust)

5

1

Post-Second World War Recovery

Having already established with his brother Reginald a successful network of dealerships in the UK in which to sell their cars and trucks, in 1936, Billy Rootes with his son Geoffrey, extensively travelled the world, taking in the Far East, the Indian subcontinent, China, Japan, the United States and Canada, seeking out new markets and hoping to identify countries with large enough potential sales growth to consider local vehicle assembly sites to boost exports. This laid the foundations of a successful motor company producing cars, vans and trucks for the world.

The Rootes factories were predominantly based in Coventry in the West Midlands. The whole city had been devastated in the war due to the concentration of industry actively involved in the war effort. Jaguar, Rover, Standard-Triumph and Armstrong-Siddeley all had manufacturing sites in and around the city and were prime targets for attack.

Prior to the war in 1936, William, or Billy as he was generally known, was approached by the government to join an industry 'Shadow Factory Scheme' committee. This was an executive group of leading motoring industrialists tasked with spearheading the production of armaments, military vehicles, aircraft (for Rootes, this primarily meant Blenheim bombers and engines) and their component parts in order to build up the country's military might as war became inevitable. The plan was to build additional factories away from existing manufacturing plants and the West Midlands.

Rootes had already set up a shadow factory at Stoke Aldermoor, adjacent to the existing factory in Humber Road, and at Ryton-on-Dunsmore to the south-east of the city. Another was Speke, near Liverpool – all of which would be less likely to be targeted for attack.

In 1937 Humber cars consisted of the '16', the Super Snipe, Snipe Imperial and the Pullman. The '16' had a 2576cc, 6-cylinder side-valve engine developing 60bhp, and the Snipe had a 3181cc, 6-cylinder side-valve developing 78bhp. A Snipe Imperial model was also introduced, which was developed to have special bodies by Thrupp & Maberly, such as the four-door Sports Saloon and Drophead Coupé. These cars were a lot more expensive to purchase; the standard Snipe retailed at £345 whereas the Snipe Imperial ranged from £495 to £555.

The Pullman and the Super Snipe used a 27HP 4086cc, 6-cylinder side-valve developing 100bhp. This was quite a powerful engine for the time and was introduced in 1935.

The origins of this engine go back to 1931, when in 2110cc and 106mm stroke form it was fitted to the Hillman Wizard, one of the first Rootes Hillmans. It was gradually developed and in 1935 ended up as the 4086cc engine with 85mm bore and 120mm stroke.

However, in-service problems with the 4086cc engine developed, such as cracked cast-iron cylinder blocks, burning valves, conrod issues and camshaft wear. Humber engineers set about making improvements to the engine and from about June 1938 introduced an improved engine that eliminated these problems. The water pump was moved to the front of the engine and belt-driven from the crankshaft pulley instead of being driven from an in-line jackshaft through the dynamo, as it had been previously.

The engine improvements were probably hastened due to the need to build up the country's military might prior to the start of the Second World War. The engine went on to be fitted to thousands of military vehicles with commendable reliability.

It served with distinction throughout the war fitted to Humber military vehicles, including Field Marshall Montgomery's famous open staff Snipe cars, the 'Old Faithful' used by him when directing the North African campaign before moving on to Italy, and the 'Victory Car' used in the European campaigns. Both cars survive and are in museums – the 'Old Faithful' resides in the Imperial War Museum in South London and the 'Victory Car' in the Coventry Transport Museum.

Thousands of saloons, limousines, armoured cars, radio trucks and personnel carriers were produced both in the UK and many overseas countries. All these vehicles, apart from the armoured cars that were designed and built separately from the car division but did use the 27HP engine, were based on the immediate pre-war 27HP Super Snipe saloon and Pullman. All were on the standard 'cruciform' 9-foot 6-inch chassis (apart from the Pullman with an extended chassis frame) with hydraulic brakes, solid rear axle and the Humber-developed and patented 'Evenkeel' front independent suspension that featured an inverted, transverse leaf spring at the front of the chassis. Sir Alec Issigonis, who went on to join Morris and later develop the iconic BMC Mini, was the engineer involved in this suspension design. Evenkeel suspension stayed on Humbers until 1952.

The government paid tribute to Billy Rootes for his tremendous efforts during the war by awarding him a knighthood in 1942.

After the war, Billy was approached by the government to arrange and send a delegation from Rootes to Volkswagen's plant in Wolfsburg, Germany, to assess the factory and establish if any of the plant could be brought back to the UK for the use of Rootes in their factories. A captured military Kubelwagen, a fully open variant of what would become the Beetle, had already been brought to Humber in 1942 to assess the design and determine whether it offered any technological advancement in motor vehicle design. A comprehensive report by Humber came to the conclusion that the vehicle offered no technological advancement in engineering practice that could be used. However, according to Geoff Carverhill in his book *The Rootes Story*, Rootes were only ever offered the plant in Germany and not the Beetle car itself.

Reginald Rootes was knighted in 1945, acknowledging his services to the war effort after serving on various manufacturing committees.

In the UK, with severe rationing still in place after the war and no finance available to develop new cars, it was a case of re-engineering pre-war designs. To energise the motor industry and to raise valuable income for the country, the post-war Labour government extolled the message to vehicle manufacturers to 'export or die'. They expected 60–70 per cent of output to be exported and Rootes took on this demanding challenge.

In 1945, a new Humber came to the market – the Mark 1 14HP (51bhp) Hawk. This was the pre-war Hillman 14 together with the 1944cc (75mm bore x 110mm stroke) side-valve 4-cylinder engine first seen in 1669cc form in 1932 in the Twelve model. New larger headlamps were fitted together with a larger boot. It had hubcaps but no wheel embellishers.

Next was the 18HP Snipe, which had the same body as the Hawk but was fitted with additional auxiliary lamps at the front. It had the 6-cylinder 2731cc (69.5mm bore x 120mm stroke) unit producing 65bhp and was introduced in 1935. Finally, there was the 27HP Super Snipe with the 4086cc, 100bhp engine. These were fitted with wheel embellishers in addition to hubcaps.

Following the war, there was no real demand for specialist coachwork for Rootes-owned coachbuilder Thrupp & Maberly, who before the war built the Pullmans as well as on-demand bespoke bodies on chassis such as Rolls-Royce and Bentley. They were based at this time in Warple Way, Acton, West London, next door to British Light Steel Pressings.

This 'outside work' now stopped and Thrupp & Maberly continued solely building the standard Pullmans, as well as specialist conversions of Pullmans for the use of the royal family and government. Later in the 1950s they also constructed the Sunbeam-Talbot 80s and later 90s. Thrupp & Maberly had been taken over by the Rootes brothers in 1925 – a very early pre-Rootes Group acquisition. This specialist division of Rootes was based, just prior to the war, in Edgware Road, moving to Warple Way in Acton, West London, before a final move back to Cricklewood in north-west London to larger premises in 1947 at the well-named Humber Road. They stayed within the Group until closure in 1968.

This 1946 advert for the post-war Humber Super Snipe emphasised how Humber vehicles were used during the conflict and could therefore be relied upon in times of peace.

However, Rootes did allow London-based coachbuilder H. J. Mulliner & Co. to construct a number of Sedanca de Ville bodies on the Pullman chassis in 1946. Externally, the only clue that it was a Humber was the retained Pullman radiator grille, bumpers and front lights. The wings and bodywork were constructed of aluminium instead of steel. Spats covered the rear wheels and, as the style of the body dictated, the roof panel above the driver was retractable into the main roof to create the 'De Ville' position. This sleek model sold for £2,300 plus purchase tax – double the price of a standard Pullman. Fifty examples were produced and today only six are known to survive.

In 1947, a Mark 2 Hawk was released introducing a new steering column-mounted gear change, a feature of the large Humbers that would stay until the end of the Hawk and Super Snipe models in 1967.

Also in 1947, both Billy and Reggie Rootes embarked on another tour of the United States. The brothers were very keen to understand and study American motor car manufacturing processes and were invited to tour the factories to see innovative manufacturing techniques and car styling so they could take ideas back to Coventry for Rootes Board consideration.

Above and right: Mulliner-bodied Pullman and interior.

9

Above and left: A CKD Mk1 Super Snipe being readied for despatch to Canada. (Richard Gruet)

Billy's oldest son Geoffrey was sent to northern Europe to establish new dealerships and his younger son Brian went to the USA later in 1947 to set up 'Rootes Incorporated' in New York. Reginald's son Timothy was in the Middle East, still on military service.

Rootes were selling cars and trucks around the world but the cost of exporting complete vehicles was very expensive for the quantities required, therefore a scheme to export 'kits' of passenger cars was devised not just by Rootes, but other manufacturers as well. Two methods were used to export cars. One involved a complete vehicle having its wheels removed and then being encased in a wooden crate and the wheels placed inside before being boxed up ready for shipping. The other process was the CKD (Completely Knocked Down) scheme, exporting body panels, trim and seating, engines, transmissions, and wheels in crates and having them assembled in Rootes-associated factories abroad.

In Australia, a site was established in a vacant military aircraft factory at Fisherman's Bend, Port Melbourne, a suburb of Melbourne, in 1947. This was where both Rootes cars and other makes were assembled. In New Zealand, a Rootes vehicle distributor, Todd Motors, based in McKenzie Street, Pentone, Wellington, had also set up a factory. They had been assembling Rootes and American Chryslers since 1936 from CKD kits sent from the UK and USA.

Australia and New Zealand had set up strict quotas on imports of cars to save overseas funds being depleted. These governments set vehicle import tariffs with licences issued to importers for set numbers of cars. Import in excess of the set numbers meant hefty tariffs added to the imported cars costs, which the importer would pass on to the customer.

The Hillman was a popular family car and demand readily outstripped supply so, to get around this, the importers badged around 40 per cent of Hillmans as Humbers, as the Humber quota was underutilised due to the cars being more expensive. There was also a requirement to ensure assembled vehicles had a certain percentage of local labour and materials, such as seating and interior materials. Therefore, parts tended to be made in these countries and fitted, satisfying those requirements. Many Mark 4 Hillman Minxes imported from 1949 onward were rebadged as the Humber Ten. Later Hillman models were badged as the 80, based on the Audax range Minx; the 90 was based on the Super Minx up to 1968; and the Singer Vogue became the Humber Vogue! Later Sceptres were imported normally.

Other popular export countries where assembly plants were established were India (Bombay); Ireland (Santry, Dublin); and, from 1949 and from 1951, Canada, South America, Japan and South Africa. The cars produced were Snipes, Super Snipes and Hawks, plus other Rootes vehicles. Eventually, by 1954, Rootes would be exporting to 132 countries around the world.

In 1949, Sir William Rootes became Chairman of the 'Dollar Exports Board' to help reorganise this department for the government. It was an advisory service for UK exporting companies, helping them to establish 'dollar' overseas markets such as the USA, Canada and countries whose currency was the dollar, which Sir William had great expertise in.

Rootes generated profits of around £1.5 million in 1945, but this was to almost halve when the development of the next generation of Humber models got underway from 1946. At that time, Rootes had around 10.9 per cent of the UK market.

2

The Mark Cars

Engineering and car design at Humber was under the control of Bernard 'BB' Winter, who had been at Rootes since 1935. Under his leadership the engineering was considered to be 'conservative' with no radical thinking, the understanding being that a design had to be fully proven and reliable. There was nothing wrong with this, but it did not push boundaries.

This was one reason that Billy and Reginald Rootes wanted to introduce new manufacturing processes and designs. To this end, Billy Rootes had discussions with Raymond Loewy in the United States during his tour of the country. Loewy was at that time Chief Designer at Studebaker. He subsequently left Studebaker to set up his own

The all-new Mk3 Hawk.

independent design office. Expanding operations, a UK-based Loewy design office was established near Rootes HQ in central London in 1939. The office was run by American stylist Clare Hodgman, assisted by Tucker Madawick. Their team liaised with Ted White, who was Head of Styling at the Stoke HQ in Coventry and assisted by Ted Green. These two men were hugely important within Rootes, designing the cars that today are so familiar.

'Full-width' styling was being seen on a number of post-war cars and one of the first designs for Humber using this style was the all-new Mk3 Hawk in September 1948. Gone were the old-style 'crocodile' bonnet and separate wings and in came a full-width style at the front with a rather jelly mould-like four-light body, which was styled similarly to the all-new Mk3 Hillman Minx. The Minx was also styled by Ted White's team with input from Tucker Madawick from the Loewy London Studio. The interior had new leather-covered bench seats and a larger glass area. The steering column gear change introduced with the previous Mk2 Hawk was retained so three people could sit in comfort on the front bench seat. The 1944cc side-valve engine from the Mk2 was also used.

The 1944cc engine was originally developed in 1932 and had a 110mm stroke and 69.5mm bore, as well as a three-bearing crankshaft with a cast-iron block and cylinder head. It was fitted to the Humber Twelve model of 1932 and had a capacity of 1669cc. This base engine was to serve Rootes and Humber well, lasting into the 1980s in various developed forms. For the Hillman 14 in 1938, it was then bored out to 75mm to increase capacity to 1944cc, producing 51bhp.

The Mk3 Hawk had an entirely new chassis, which was slightly shorter than the previous model. Handling was improved by the provision of an independent coil spring suspension and anti-roll bar at the front and conventional leaf springs at the rear. The car retailed at £799. However, it was still deemed to be underpowered and so in September 1950 was superseded by the Mk4, where the engine was bored out again to 81mm. This made for a 2267cc capacity but retained a side-valve configuration. Output power was 58bhp. This gave improved performance, better fuel economy and acceleration. Small side lights were fitted below the headlamps, but beyond this the body and interior remained the same.

Meanwhile, the Mk1 Super Snipe, like the Mk1 and Mk2 Hawk, also carried over the 1939 design of a six-light saloon – a large boot bustle, narrow-width running boards, larger headlamps, fog and spot lamps, and the Evenkeel independent front suspension. The engine was the long-lived 4086cc 6-cylinder side-valve engine.

The Mk1 Super Snipe was popular with the police due to the powerful engine and well-appointed interior. The Metropolitan Police in London had a fleet. The car enjoyed good publicity by featuring in the 1950 Ealing Studios film *The Blue Lamp*, featuring prominently in the opening title sequences shot on the Harrow Road in West London.

An interesting aside is that all government cabinet ministers in 1947 were issued with Mk1 Super Snipes as their official cars.

A Mk1 Snipe model was also introduced, the car having the same body as the Super Snipe but being fitted with the slightly less powerful 18HP 2731cc 6-cylinder engine, which developed 65bhp. It retained a floor gear change lever; otherwise the specification was the same.

The post-war Hawks, Snipes and Super Snipes were popular with the public and police forces around the UK and the chassis was made available so that a wide range of

The Mk1 Super Snipe as used in the 1950 Ealing Studios film *The Blue Lamp*, starring Jack Warner as PC George Dixon.

coach-built options, generally for the Super Snipe, could be fitted. These included hearses, ambulances, newspaper delivery vehicles and open pick-ups that were only available to the oil industry in the Middle East.

For 1948, the Loewy influence was evident in the redesign of the Pressed Steel body of the Super Snipe, introducing a more modern look for the Mk2. The headlamps were now built into the wings with auxiliary lamps below and the wings were moulded to meet the crocodile-style bonnet. Intriguingly, the six-light body was *retained*, but was widened by some 5½ inches (140mm) to increase the internal width for driver and passenger so that a bench seat could be fitted to accommodate three people. The chassis was lengthened by 7 inches (178mm). Running boards were reintroduced with ribbed rubber along their length. The 'suicide' style opening front doors (hinged at the rear) were retained.

The Mk2 was launched at the 1948 Earls Court Motor Show but the slower-selling Mk1 Snipe with the 2731cc engine was dropped from the line-up, with only 1,240 cars sold. The Mk2 had full leather seating, wood veneer dashboard and door cappings. Column gear change was introduced to this model following the Mk2 Hawk, which introduced this feature. Although considered a luxury car, a heater and radio were optional.

1948 was a busy year for Humber as the new Pullman was released in May, with production starting in September 1947. The body was made by Thrupp & Maberly, Rootes' own coachbuilder now based in Cricklewood. The front end styling followed that of the Mk2 Super Snipe, but from the 'A' posts back it was entirely new. The 4086cc engine was mated to the standard four-speed gearbox, with column-mounted gear change, to bring the car in line with other Humber models. Mounted on the 10-foot 11-inch (3.33m) chassis, it

Above and below: An Experimental Department mock-up of a design for the new 1948 Mk2 Super Snipe, and an early production car.

had the standard rear-hinged front doors and the conventional forward-hinged rears with additional side windows, making it a six-light design. The doors were of a full-height design that swept out at the bottom, thus the previous model's step boards were eliminated. Inside, the glazed partition was mounted in a framework on the front seat that was limited in its free movement. The driver's area had leather on the front bench seat, whereas in the rear

West of England cloth was used for the seat trimming as an alternative to leather – though leather was still available as an option. Two occasional fold-up seats were provided, which folded up against the partition. Heating was provided for the rear passengers, and as an option a radio could be installed with the control unit built into the rear-offside armrest.

The boot had an unusual push-button arrangement for opening the pull-down boot lid (a Thrupp & Maberly-patented design) to access the luggage storage area. The boot lid could also be utilised to have luggage strapped down on it. Inside, the glass division was in two halves and slid horizontally. On the bonnet was a simple chrome plain motif.

The Pullman was almost the standard official car for governments both in the UK and overseas, and was used for civic duties and by heads of state around the world. It was a highly successful car in this sector of the market, surviving to 1954.

In 1949, another version of the Pullman was introduced – the Imperial. This resurrected a Humber model name last used between 1937 and 1939. The primary difference between this model and the Pullman was the loss of the glazed partition and the West of England cloth on the rear seats being replaced by leather. The occasional seats were retained and it was targeted for the owner/driver who might want to transport eight people in comfort.

The Mk2 Super Snipe and Pullman chassis were quite adaptable and, as seen with the MK1, could be supplied to coachbuilders to be produced as hearses or ambulances. Super Snipes were even used as box vans by a number of newspaper printers to deliver papers

An advert image depicting the new Mk2 Pullman crossing Parliament Square by Big Ben with important MPs inside, but not the chauffeur, who had the 'A' pillar across his face! A painting by Frank Wootton.

around London and other UK cities. For this duty, the vehicles were supplied with rubber front wings and had the main headlights mounted in-board on steel pillars either side of the radiator grille, with a fairly rudimentary wood-framed steel-panelled body. The *London Evening News* hired a fleet of these vehicles from United Services Transport to carry out this arduous work. A chap I spoke with some years ago was a boy on the Saturday evening runs when the 'Football Final Results' were released. So anxious were people to know the results, it meant a fast run out of Fleet Street to all around London. But for him, it was a trip across South London to Croydon dropping off bundles of 'Late Finals' to newsagents by the road or to shops at breakneck speeds! He clearly remembers one journey when his Humber van overtook a police car on a call, so determined were they to get the deliveries done!

The script on the sides of the bonnet changed depending on what the chassis/vehicle was destined to become. For standard cars it was 'Super Snipe', 'Pullman' or 'Imperial' scripts but for non-standard body types it was simply 'Humber'.

Rootes were very keen to attract Royal patronage and was honoured to be chosen to supply specialist cars for home and overseas royal visits and tours. Humber was favoured by King George V and VI, the Duke of Windsor, our present Queen, Queen Elizabeth II, and the Queen Mother over the years.

Evening News Mk2 Super Snipe vans being readied for newspaper deliveries. Note that the front wings were rubber to cope with odd knocks. (Solo Syndication)

Above and below: The specially built royal tour duty Mk2 Pullmans by Thrupp & Maberly.

With the introduction of the Mk2 Pullman in 1948, the opportunity was taken by Thrupp & Maberly to develop alternative body styles to compete with Rolls-Royce and Daimler. In 1951, Humber was given a contract to supply cars to Australia for a planned royal tour by King George VI in 1952. Twenty-six Humbers consisting of a Pullman Landaulette and a specially equipped Pullman; twelve standard Pullmans; and twelve of the brand-new Mk4 Super Snipes were shipped out for the intended state visit.

Regrettably, the king passed away in February 1952 and the tour was cancelled. Later, a new tour was planned and went ahead in 1954 with the newly crowned Queen Elizabeth and her husband, the Duke of Edinburgh, using the cars already sent out in 1948 and 1952.

Above and below: The newly crowned Queen Elizabeth II with her husband the Duke of Edinburgh on their tour of Australia in 1954.

The cars stayed in Australia/New Zealand and were sold off locally some years later. Most disappeared but a few survived and one example was the subject of a major restoration and shipped out to the Pacific island of Tonga for the use of King Tupou VI for his coronation on 4 July 2015.

1949 saw a collaboration with Tickford coachbuilders of Newport Pagnell in Buckinghamshire to develop an attractive two-door coupé on the Mk2 Super Snipe chassis. A contract was entered into with Humber providing Mk2 Super Snipe chassis

Above and left: The Tickford-bodied Mk2 Super Snipe and a body under construction in Tickford's factory.

The Tickford Super Snipe previously owned by Vernon Cox.

for Tickford to produce some 124 examples from August 1949 until production ended in July 1950. The car featured two elongated saloon doors with the bodywork formed over an ash frame. Access to the rear seats was granted by the front seats having an off-set tip forward seat squab. The hood could be placed in three positions, fully enclosed, de Ville, or fully retracted. The rear of the body was completely new with restyled wings and large curved boot lid and rear wheel spats. They sold for £1,993, equivalent to around £68,000 in 2020.

In 1950, a subtle change was made to the Mk2 with the introduction of smaller side lamps below the headlamps replacing the larger auxiliary circular lamps. Internally the car was referred to as the Mk2A. With this attractive body style and unique tie-up with Tickford, around twenty-nine examples still exist around the world in the hands of enthusiasts. The data the Club holds was compiled by enthusiast Club member Vernon Cox, who owned a superbly restored example.

Another unusual version of the Super Snipe was a two-door pick-up truck produced for the oil industry in the Middle East, who needed heavy-duty, rugged support vehicles. A Mk1 had already been produced in 1947 by coachbuilder Reale of Ealing, West London, and so testing of the Mk2 chassis in 1948 was started prior to production on the Mk3 and later the Mk4 chassis. There was a simple drop-down tailgate supported by chains. Almost two-thirds of the length of the vehicle was the bonnet, engine and cab – leaving only a third for carrying any load! It is thought that the all-steel pick-up body was supplied by Hawson of Sunbury-on-Thames, Middlesex. Armstrong-Siddeley had also produced a small run of this type of vehicle as well. Excellent reproduction examples of an Mk2 and Mk4 Super Snipe pick-up can be seen in the Isle of Man Motor Museum.

For 1950, Rootes set about steady improvements across the model range.

HUMBER SUPER-SNIPE

STATION WAGON AND PICK-UP

Above and below: Brochure for the Mk3 estate and pick-up versions of the Super Snipe. This body style was used up to the Mk4 Super Snipe, which is also shown. These would have been special orders.

The Pullman and Imperial models became the Mk3 by having subtle changes made to the rear suspension, such as a Panhard rod to better control 'roll'. The scalloped front and rear bumpers were changed to rounded ones with new over-riders and small side lights below the headlamps replacing the previous circular auxiliary lamps.

There was a market in specialised vehicles such as estate versions, where the Snipes and Pullmans were generally not supplied from Humber. Some examples were, however, produced by specialist coachbuilders in limited numbers. Tickford, who had constructed the coupés, produced an estate with external wood framing. 'MXK 781', as it was registered, was a demonstrator mounted on a Mk3 Pullman chassis. I clearly remember seeing this actual car in an Essex breaker's yard in the 1980s, scrapped. Such a shame. Another Mk3 Pullman received a similarly styled coachwork from Warwick Coachbuilders – external wooden trim featured on the doors and rear – again as a one-off, but fortunately this car still exists. Other coachbuilders were also able to provide bespoke estate versions on either chassis on request.

In 1950, the Mk3 Super Snipe was launched, which had some superficial styling changes over the Mk2 and improvements to the suspension. Still utilising the Evenkeel independent front suspension, the transverse spring was doubled in width from 2½ inches (65mm) to 5 inches (140mm) but the number of leaves was reduced from fifteen to eight. A Panhard rod was added to the rear suspension to improve handling, as per the Pullman. The rear boot lid was redesigned with the removal of the rear lights, which were transferred to the wings, leaving just the number plate in position. Although running boards were retained, two new individual alloy steps with ribbed rubber sections were provided below the front and rear door on each side. With a nod to transatlantic styling,

The country estate on the Mk3 Pullman chassis by Tickford.

The 1952 Mk3 Super Snipe. This example was owned for sixty years by Club member John Easton and is now owned by the author, his son-in-law.

the rear wheels had spats fitted over them that had a turn-key mechanism for removal to provide wheel access. A 'Snipe' bird motif adorned the bonnet, which now received a new raised edge to the bonnet line on both sides adjacent to the wings. This makes distinguishing between the Mk2 and 3 Super Snipes and Pullmans easier. The Mk3 was priced at £1,144, or £1,240 for a limousine version with an adjustable glazed division between the front and rear compartments. A valve radio was extra. Around 17,000 examples of the Mk2 and Mk3 Super Snipe were produced.

With the 1951 Festival of Britain being celebrated around the country, Princess Elizabeth, prior to becoming Queen, embarked on many events around the UK to celebrate the occasion. One such city to host an event was Norwich. The main Rootes dealer in that city, the Norwich Motor Company, arranged with Humber to supply cars for taking the princess around the city. Humber supplied one of the Royal Tour Mk2 Pullman Landaulettes and several other Pullmans. The Chief Constable of Norfolk had a Mk4 Hawk, which was the lead car for journeys around the city. Fortunately, many photographs were taken to record the event and some are reproduced here.

In 1952, for the Summer Olympics held in the Finnish capital Helsinki, Humber delivered an order for 200 Mk4 Hawks for use as officials cars. Some of these cars are still in existence today.

The Hawk was now due an upgrade and so a new, slightly larger body was launched as the Mk5 in September 1952. It received a new body and retained its vertical grille, although this was restyled with new chromed side grilles incorporating side lights. The body was some 6 inches longer. It retained the 2267cc side-valve engine of 58bhp and retailed at £650.

Before being crowned Queen, Princess Elizabeth embarked on a tour of Britain as part of the 1951 'Festival of Britain' celebrations. These photographs show her visiting Norwich in Norfolk in one of the Royal Tour Landaulettes.

Above and below: The Mk5 Hawk.

Finally, the last of the Hawks with a separate chassis, the Mk6 Hawk, launched in October 1952. It had an overhead valve version of the previously used 2267cc side-valve engine. First seen in the Sunbeam-Talbot 90, this engine had increased power output from 58bhp to 70bhp. The body was essentially the same but now featured vertical rear light units, as used on the Alvis TD21 and Aston-Martin DB4. A trim strip was added to the side of the front wings, which extended along the driver and passenger doors. Overdrive was offered as a transmission option along with a radio and heater.

The design of a new Super Snipe had been developed since 1950 with a view to superseding the six-light body. Advantage was taken of the Mk4 Hawk bodyshell by extending the basic design to develop a prototype. A new overhead valve 6-cylinder engine was available, designed by Arthur Booth OBE (the commendation was given to him for developing Humber armoured cars during the Second World War) and developed after the war by Commer to replace the venerable 4086cc side-valve unit that had been around since 1935. They had developed two sizes of the engine – a 4750cc engine with 3¾-inch cylinder bores, horizontally mounted under-cab floor in the QX truck, and another of 4139cc with 3½-inch cylinder bores. This unit produced 113bhp at 3400rpm. In the car division, the engine was known as the 'Blue Ribbon', carrying a transfer on the rocker box to say so. The name is thought to refer to a competition on the transatlantic passenger run for the passenger ship that could cross the fastest between Southampton and New York, with a Blue Ribbon award given to the fastest liner. Great Britain was the Blue Ribbon holder for many years with the *Queen Mary* and *Queen Elizabeth* ships.

In 1986 I was privileged to meet Bill Hancock, Director and General Manager of the Rootes Coventry factories employing over 10,000 staff in the 1950s. He told me of early developments in testing the new OHV engine in a converted Mk4 Hawk in early 1951. As the Hawk body could not accommodate the new engine, the front of the car and chassis were redesigned and extended by 12 inches (305mm) and given flared wheel arches to accommodate the larger 7.00 x 15 cross-ply tyres. This new front end was produced by Briggs Motor Bodies Ltd of Dagenham, Essex, who supplied Ford with car bodies for the adjacent factory and were part of this organisation.

Bill Hancock and his wife embarked on an extensive tour with the prototype driving down through France and Italy, including routes taken in Monte Carlo rally stages, in order to test the performance of the new engine. Photographs Bill and his wife took of the car are shown here. Further design work was carried out to encompass a larger boot, making it look a well-balanced design. A new chassis was designed that was some 10 inches (25cm) longer than the Mk3. The 'Super Snipe' script was placed on the front wings adjacent to the front doors. The basic saloon retailed at £985.

The Rootes organisation were very keen on publicity for the various marques in their portfolio and Humber was no exception. To publicise the introduction of the Mk4 Super Snipe, two endurance events were arranged – one managed by the Competitions Department, the other by a member of the public already known to Rootes.

Norman Garrad was Rootes Competition Manager and was highly successful in this role, going on to ensure Rootes cars, notably Sunbeam-Talbots, Rapiers and later Alpine and Tiger cars, were used in rallies around the world. Sales were bolstered by the publicity that came with these events. Humbers were not thought of as rallying cars, but a few had done exceptionally well. One such event was when the respected Dutch rally driver Maurice

Above and below: Here Bill Hancock and his wife take the Mk4 Super Snipe development car on a European trip. (E.W. Hancock)

Gatsonides nearly won the 1949 Monte Carlo rally in a Mk2 Super Snipe, finishing second. Norman was asked to develop a special endurance journey to launch the Mk4. He and his team devised a route that would entail the car driving through as many European countries in the quickest possible time.

The assembled team included Stirling Moss, who was already a driver for the Sunbeam-Talbot team, John Cutts, Leslie Johnson and David Humphrey, who were brought together to take on this rather unusual trial. The plan was to start in Norway then travel through Sweden, Denmark, Germany, Holland, Belgium, Luxembourg, France, Switzerland, Liechtenstein, Austria, Italy, Yugoslavia, Monaco, Spain and ending in Portugal. The Mk4 chosen was straight from the production line with no special rallying features for speed or comfort. Starting in Norway on 2 December 1952 at 02.00 in the morning, they arrived in Lisbon in a record 3 days, 17 hours and 59 minutes! A stunning performance that won acclaim for the team, and especially the new Mk4 Humber Super Snipe.

However, a second even more ambitious event was in the planning stage. This involved a Yorkshire adventurer, George Hinchliffe from Bradford. A garage owner, George had organised a previous overland journey to Cape Town in South Africa using an old Austin van converted to a motorhome in 1948. In 1949 he had got the journey time down to 24 days, 2 hours and 50 minutes with an Austin A70. However, in 1950 George undertook the same trip with a Mk4 Hillman Minx and completed the journey in 22 days. Rootes were aware of these achievements and thought getting George to take a brand-new car off the production line to try and beat the previous record, demonstrating the strength and reliability of the car, would be the perfect way to publicise the launch of the Mk4

Rear shot of the Mk4 Super Snipe during its 'fifteen countries in ninety hours' endurance run driven by Stirling Moss, Leslie Johnson and John Cutts.

Super Snipe. Norman Garrad and the Rootes Competition Department assisted George by prepping the car, arranging the publicity (the journey was filmed in colour throughout) and giving support as required.

For this endurance run, George had Robbie Walshaw and Arthur Longman with him. They assembled with the heavily loaded car at Hyde Park, London, on 26 November 1952 at 10.15 a.m., together with Rootes officials and the press. They set off for Lympne Aerodrome on the Kent Coast to be loaded onto a Silver City Airways Bristol Freighter aircraft flying to Le Touquet in France to continue the journey. They drove down to Marseilles then took a ferry to Algiers. An arduous journey over the Atlas Mountains brought them to the Sahara Desert. This section over the desert was some 2,337 miles and the group encountered many problems, including getting bogged down in soft sand – requiring digging out – and puncturing the petrol tank, which necessitated the emptying of the fresh water containers to fill with petrol so fuel could be piped to the carburettor. A gruelling journey through jungles and swamps of French Equatorial Africa then followed. On arrival in Cape Town they sent a cable to Rootes HQ in Devonshire House, London, to advise of their arrival in a remarkable 13 days, 9 hours and 6 minutes, covering some 10,500 miles – a record that stood for many years.

Even in Australia, the Mk4 was utilised to demonstrate its strength and reliability with no fewer than five cars entered into the Redex Round-Australia Reliability Trial in August

Above and opposite: The Mk4 Super Snipe's ambitious endurance run from London to Cape Town, South Africa, in 1952. Pictured are Arthur Longman, Robbie Walshaw and George Hinchliffe at the start at Hyde Park, and in the Sahara Desert. The run was achieved in just over thirteen days.

1953 – covering some 6,500 very rugged miles. Five Super Snipes were entered, comprising three from the main Rootes dealer in Sydney and two independents, with 192 cars of various makes undertaking this daunting journey. One of the Rootes-sponsored cars came second overall and also won 'Best in Class for over 2500cc'. An outstanding success.

With further overseas royal tours being organised, Humber were required to supply suitable cars. Ten Mk4 Super Snipe cars were chosen with four saloons being made into convertibles by H. J. Mulliner of London. There were a number of special features fitted including radios and special blinds that allegedly the Duke of Edinburgh designed to protect the Queen's knees against sunburn! At least two of these cars were sent to Australia, Ceylon and Gibraltar for tours in 1954. Fortunately, one genuine car has been brought back to the UK from Australia and can be seen on display in the marvellous Isle of Man Motor Museum.

The Mk4A Super Snipe was introduced in October 1953 with an external difference being the extended stainless trim on the front doors covering almost the width of the door. Engine power was increased slightly from 113bhp to 116bhp through the use of a revised cylinder head to increase the compression ratio.

A year later, the Mk4B Super Snipe entered showrooms. This brought about some American influences with the option of two-tone paint schemes with a chrome strip around the body at window level as the dividing line between the colours. Rootes had already trialled this successfully with Hillman and the 'Gay Look' Mk8 Minx for 1955 offering several two-tone colour schemes. The Mk4B Super Snipe also saw the introduction of a wood veneer dashboard and door cappings, improved seating (with individual seats available as an option), and the boot-mounted number plate was set within a plinth

Left and below: The Mk4 Super Snipe conversion by H. J. Mulliner of London. It was used on royal tours in 1954 to Australia, Ceylon and Gibraltar. Here we see the car being assembled by Ceylonese staff and then on tour in Ceylon.

Above and right: A special
Mk4 Super Snipe supplied to
the Duke of Windsor for his
in-exile home in Paris – the
picture was signed by him for
Humber. An interior view of
the rear shows a reduced-size
rear window modified by
Thrupp & Maberly.

moulded to the shape of the boot lid. Overdrive was offered along with automatic transmission using a Borg-Warner DG gearbox.

The Mk4 Super Snipe could also be ordered as an estate but the number produced was very limited. Due to its size, the BBC used some as mobile radio broadcasting vehicles as the weight of the equipment that needed to be carried was no problem. Like previous Super Snipes, this model could be supplied as a chassis for coachbuilders to build bodies such as ambulances and hearses. Production ended in 1957 with some 18,000 examples being built.

Following the duo-tone paintwork phase, the final version of the Mk6 Hawk launched in 1956 as the Mk6A. This was also offered with these paint schemes as well as single tones. The Hawk also had the wood veneer dash and door cappings. A Laycock overdrive was an option, but not automatic transmission.

THE NEW

HUMBER HAWK

DE LUXE SALOON

The Mk6A Hawk.

Like the Mk4 Super Snipe, an estate car was also added. This featured a split tailgate where the glazed upper half lifted up and the tailgate hinged down to provide a flat platform.

The Pullman and Imperial also received the 4139cc OHV engine in 1953, becoming the Mk4, but only lasted until the following year. The market for these large Humbers was coming to an end with other limousines such as the Austin Princess and those produced by Daimler filling the gap, so production ended the following year in 1954 with only 414 examples being manufactured. This brought to an end a prestigious lineage dating back to 1935. So, was this the end for the Pullman model? Possibly not.

Although not confirmed, the Club has in its archive pictures of an unusual Pullman with a relatively modern body from the 'A' post rearward. This car can be seen in an assumed publicity shot and also with Sir William Rootes entering it with his wife on his way to his investiture at Buckingham Palace in January 1959 to receive his title of Lord Rootes of Ramsbury (Wiltshire), where he had a magnificent manor house and estate. Carrying a Coventry registration issued in May 1954 the car was dispatched to Devonshire House, London, on 30 July, and from the records of manufacture was the second to last Pullman to be produced. The current consensus is that it may have been bodied by Hooper and could have been a prototype for a new generation of Pullman, but this cannot be confirmed. The car does still exist and there are plans to try and recover it in the future.

However, the age of cars having a separate chassis was coming to an end. The next generation of Humber was starting to take shape.

3

The Series Cars

Toward the middle of the 1950s, the Humber design office started work on the next generation of Humber and looked to the United States for inspiration. The design would become the last truly designed Humber car and would have a ten-year lifespan once the Hawk went on sale in May 1957. It would also see the same basic body style utilised for both the Hawk and the Super Snipe. The Hawk would retain the 2267cc 4-cylinder engine with some technical changes. Once developed, a new 6-cylinder engine was utilised for the Super Snipe.

Working under Rootes Engineering Director Bernard 'BB' Winter, the established styling team headed up by Ted White, assisted by Ted Green, started with a blank sheet of paper. The use of a separate chassis was being superseded by unitary construction in the motor industry, where a sub-frame would support the engine, transmission, steering and suspension with the rear suspension and axle attached to the body direct. This allowed a much lower bodyline to be achieved as well as leading to weight savings. Sir William and Sir Reginald Rootes were very keen on how designs in America were evolving, and so another contract was drawn up with the London Loewy office, under Clare Hodgman, to assist with ideas on how the new design of body should look. Around 1955 a quarter-scale clay model was produced by Clare ostensibly as a Hillman Minx, a development of the new Audax range of Rootes cars, but it is clear that the design embodies what would become the new Series Hawk.

A poor image of a potential Hillman Minx by Clare Hodgman of London-based Loewy Design, which would go on to form the basis of the new Series car.

THE "ONE-FIFTY" 4-DOOR SEDAN

You get "show car" beauty in Chevrolet's lowest-priced series,
too! Take this "One-Fifty" 4-Door Sedan, for example, with its
fresh, clean lines . . . its handsome, comfortable interior. What
a wonderful way to go thrifty!

THE BEL AIR 4-DOOR STATION WAGON

Above and left: Styling cues for the Series cars, as exemplified on the Chevrolet 150 Series saloon and estate car of 1955.

Key features seemed to follow American design practice seen on the second generation Chevrolet 150/210 series introduced in 1954, and to have been incorporated into the new Hawk. There were deep section bumpers with over-riders, upsweep on the rear doors, and a dog-leg design of the front doors to improve access and wrap-around front and rear screens.

Once a design had been signed off, Northampton company Airflow Streamlines were commissioned to build prototype unitary construction bodies for structural testing. At this time, the car was to have one of the largest unitary bodyshells in the United Kingdom.

The original plan was to launch the new Hawk and Super Snipe together in 1957, but delays in developing an all-new 6-cylinder engine saw the Super Snipe postponed for a year. The cars would be assembled in the Ryton plant with the bodies being produced by Rootes company British Light Steel Pressings in Acton, West London, next to where Thrupp & Maberly were located before their move to new premises in the specially named Humber Road, Cricklewood. Engines, gearboxes (except automatic transmissions) and back axles were made and assembled at the Stoke plant in Coventry.

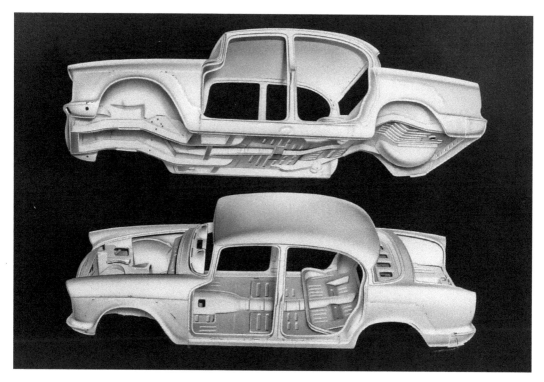

The monocoque body of the Series model, one of the largest in Britain at the time.

Prototypes were built during 1956 with extensive testing undertaken on test routes developed by Rootes that covered the UK and Europe. A lot of testing was undertaken at the relatively new MIRA (Motor Industry Research Association) facility near Nuneaton, where high-speed tracks including banked circuits, Belgian pave roads, dust tunnels, adverse camber road and gradient circuits were located.

A cross-section of the Series 1 Hawk.

Above and left: Publicity images of the Series 1 Hawk.

Three variants were to be available – saloon, estate and a touring limousine. The limousine was created with a frame built into the rear of the front bench seat, which was in contact with the 'B' pillars and the roof to form an acoustic seal. A glass panel slid up and down on runners within the frame. The whole seat unit could still be moved back and forth to suit the driver.

Using the monocoque shell gave a weight saving of some 100 pounds (45.3kgs) over its predecessor, the Mk6 Hawk.

Looking at the technical aspects, the Hawk engine carried over was the 2267cc 4-cylinder unit used on the Mk5 and Mk6 Hawks and Mk3 Sunbeam-Talbot 90s, but would have a slightly higher power output of 78bhp at 4400rpm. To attain a low bonnet line, the distributor that was mounted centrally along the cylinder head on the Mk6 Hawk was relocated to the front, lower down and at an angle with an alternative skew drive on the camshaft. The engine had a new casting to locate the distributor's new position. It now brought the distributor cap below the level of the rocker box cover.

At the front, a sub-frame was designed to mount the engine and suspension, which featured unequal-length wishbones, coil springs and integral dampers. Newly introduced to the motor industry, Metallastic engine mounts (rubber and steel sections bonded together) were used extensively for engine, gearbox and propeller shaft support to reduce vibration, and Metallastic bushes were used in the attachment of the rear leaf springs to the body and the axle casing.

However, Humber still continued to use threaded pins and bushes on the front suspension, which required periodic greasing. In fact, there were no fewer than twenty-seven grease nipples on the suspension and drivetrain – these required greasing every 1,000 miles!

Transmission was a four-speed synchromesh gearbox, except first, and retained steering column gear change. Therefore, apart from the transmission tunnel, this allowed three adults to sit in comfort across the leather-covered front bench seat – although individual seats were offered as an option, with both versions having armrests. A three-speed automatic Borg-Warner DG gearbox was also an option, as was a Laycock overdrive unit working on third and fourth gears. Drum brakes were fitted all around as servo-assisted disc-braking systems were, at this time, still under development. Tyres were 640 x 15 cross-plies.

An 11.5-gallon fuel tank was provided, which had a unique feature regarding the filling of the tank. Without wanting to add a petrol filler cap on the flanks of the rear wings, it was decided to mount the filler behind the off-side reflector of the right-hand rear light cluster to fill the tank located under the boot floor. Thus the reflector was rotated and removed to expose the filler pipe. This feature caught out many owners and petrol station attendants!

Colour schemes were either four single tone or five duo tone. For the latter, one colour covered below the waist trim and roof with the second colour from the roof guttering to the waist stainless steel trim. The waist trim dropped down to the wrap-around bumper on the rear wings.

Although wooden dashboards were fitted in previous Humbers, unusually this new Hawk did not. It instead had a metal 'wood effect' dashboard and plain painted metal above the door panel trims. There was, however, a padded top to the dash. Initially the bonnet release was external, being encompassed in the top bar of the radiator grille but later changed to a pull cable below the dash on the driver's side.

For instrumentation, there were two primary dials: a speedometer and a combined triple-gauge unit that showed engine temperature but blanked for oil pressure and dynamo output charge. These latter two were optional extras and so the car was supplied with the wording 'HUMBER' and 'HAWK' in each sector. The petrol gauge was mounted centrally between the two main gauges.

Centrally, there were two rotary switches – one for ventilation the other for the external lights. A clock was between the two. The heater was an option and had its rotary control on the fascia to the lower right of the steering column.

Oddments could be kept in the glovebox or the cubby holes set into the door panels. Pile carpeting was fitted throughout on the saloons, but was rubber on the estates except on the transmission tunnel as these were deemed to be 'utility' vehicles.

The car launched in May 1957 to great acclaim with the estate car following in October of the same year, in time for the annual London Motor Show at Earls Court. The new Hawk retailed at £1,261 for the saloon, £1,381 for the limousine and £1,463 for the estate.

Complete cars were exported, but in certain territories it was cheaper to despatch vehicles from the UK as CKD (Completely Knocked Down) kits of body panels, mechanical parts and some trim. This also allowed more cars to be exported, and territories to benefit from this approach included Australia and New Zealand. At Port Melbourne, Australia, assembly tracks were in place to build the cars. Import tariffs were relatively high and the Australian government also required that as much local content be incorporated into the assembly. Hawks and Super Snipes sent built-up were generally painted in the standard colours of the UK, but CKDs were also painted in light colours such as white, yellow, light green and blue in order to deflect the strong sun's rays and

An Australian-built
Series 2 Hawk
with 'local
colour scheme'.
(Rick Cefai)

help reduce the car's inside temperature. External sun visors were popular options. Complete built-up export cars and CKD cars were identified by their chassis number and lettering. There are details at the end of the book, but in general HSO defined a UK-built home car as 'H' = Home, 'S' = Saloon ('U' = Estate, 'L' = Limousine), 'O' = ordinary/standard specification. For CKD-assembled cars the first letter was 'W', which stood for right-hand drive CKD, or 'X' for left-hand drive CKD.

Not many UK manufacturers of large saloons had tackled the production of an estate car, but Humber did. Once more, there was a leaning toward how Chevrolet had designed estates – known as station wagons in the USA. The Humber, almost identically to the Chevrolet Series 150/210 Bel-Air estate/station wagons, would have a split tailgate arrangement with a glazed upper half that lifted up and a pull-down tailgate. There were wrap-around rear side windows to meet the tailgate assembly. This design added structural rigidity to the rear of the car. When the tailgate was pulled down to the horizontal position, it provided a platform for loading into the car or to sit on. The rear seat simply folded down by operating an enclosed chain on the rear of the seat to release latches each side. This gave a flat load space up to the back of the front seats – some 5 feet (1.5m) in length.

The front doors were standard, but the rear doors had their upper sections cut and made square rather than curving like the saloon door. This suited the estate profile. All estates had rubber flooring front and rear instead of carpet, as it was assumed all cars would be used by owners with muddy boots! Carpet was retained over the transmission tunnel.

The first estates had the rear number plate mounted on the body below the tailgate and lit by a lamp on the bumper. Reversing lamps were each side. A removable floor panel in the load space was opened by releasing two latches with a special key provided, revealing the spare wheel, jacking equipment and storage area.

The exhaust rear tailpipe was also altered. On the saloons, the tailpipe came out from under the body just to the right of centre. During testing, it was found that exhaust fumes

A Series 1 Hawk in the showroom of Rootes dealer George Hartwell of Bournemouth. (Rootes Archive Centre Trust)

were entering the car when driving, so for both the Hawk and Super Snipes the exhaust pipe was redesigned to exit under the right-hand corner of the body to eradicate the problem.

Estate cars were obviously a lower-volume production model. This would interfere with production of not just Humber saloon cars but also other Rootes cars in Ryton. So the estates were assembled initially at Singer's now redundant factory in Birmingham using partly built-up saloon bodies from BLSP in London. However, space was at a premium here and Rootes looked to outsource the building of the estate cars to another Coventry company, Carbodies Ltd. This company, based in Holyhead Road, was used by a number of motor firms such as Daimler and BMC for undertaking vehicle production, including the FX3 and FX4 Austin/BMC taxis for London and other cities and for Ford, making the Mk2 Zephyr and Zodiac convertibles. But Carbodies themselves were also extremely short of space and were desperately looking for an additional manufacturing site. The old Lancaster bomber repair hangar at Baginton airfield just outside the city was available and so a lease was taken to use this facility. When the Humber estate contract was let, all the manufacturing jigs from the old Singer factory in Birmingham moved there together with the prepared bodyshells from BLSP to build the complete car and paint them. The cars returned to Humber for fitting of the mechanical components. Production eventually reached twenty cars a week until it ceased in 1967. In parallel to the Humbers, Carbodies would go on to produce estates for Hillman and Singer as well.

A feather in the cap for Carbodies came in 1961 when they won an IBCAM Gold medal for the Super Snipe Series 3 estate car at the Earl's Court Motor Show.

Rover looked at the Humber and had a Super Snipe estate in for evaluation. In 1959, Pressed Steel built an estate on a P5 3-litre chassis but could not achieve the structural rigidity at the back that the Humber possessed, and it was allegedly said by a Rover engineer that Humber 'must have fitted an RSJ across the back'! Rover did not progress the idea of an estate car.

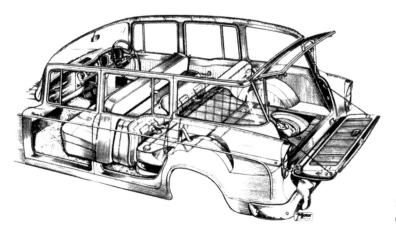

Series 1 estate car detail.

Later in 1957, the Hawk's fuel tank was increased from an 11.5-gallon capacity to 12.5 gallons, and in 1958 a walnut veneer dashboard was fitted together with wood trims along the top of the doors following customer response. These wood features would remain on the model until the end of production in 1967.

1958 also saw the emergence of the new Series 1 Super Snipe, which shared the body of the Hawk and was offered with the same body variants – saloon, limousine and estate car. But of course, the key difference was the engine.

The previous Mk4 Super Snipe had used the 4139cc 6-cylinder engine, also shared with Commer, but this was deemed to be too heavy and the fuel consumption was poor. So work started on developing a more modern engine to use the latest combustion design technology, giving a similar power output but at reduced weight, size and cost and offering improvements in fuel economy.

Although not clear on how it came about, Rootes were aware in 1952 that Armstrong-Siddeley Motors (ASM) were launching a new car – the Star Sapphire 346. This featured an all-new 3.4-litre straight 6-cylinder engine having advanced features such as a cross-flow cylinder

The Series 1 Hawk estate at the 1957 Motor Show.

head where fuel and air entered the engine on the left-hand side (as looking at the front of a car) with the exhaust on the right-hand side. Combustion was greatly improved by using 'hemispherically' shaped combustion chambers for each cylinder with inclined inlet and exhaust valves. This design derived from work undertaken in 1949 by Allard of Brixton, who were very active in motor racing, using and developing their own engines. The design they were working on aimed to produce an engine of around 125bhp in overhead valve form.

The Star Sapphire engine had 'square' bore/stroke dimensions of 90mm/3.54in and a total capacity of 3435cc with a 7:1 compression ratio. Due to the cross-flow arrangement, the cylinder head had twin rocker shafts to operate the inlet and exhaust valves operated by push rods actuated by the high-level camshaft. The spark plugs were located centrally at the bottom of steel tubes. Sound familiar?

Rootes were already working with ASM, providing them with four-speed manual gearboxes for the Star Sapphire, and thus it is assumed a contract was let for them to collaborate with Humber's engine design team to develop the new engine. Eventually a smaller-capacity engine was ready in 1957 but it was too late for a car launch with the Hawk – more testing was needed. There was also the setting up of manufacturing facilities at Rootes' Stoke plant together with Armstrong-Siddeley, who were also contracted to build the engine. However, ASM were going through major upheavals due to them now becoming part of the greater Hawker Siddeley group, and their primary business was the building of aircraft and aircraft engines. In 1959, Armstrong went on to become Bristol Siddeley Engines Ltd and continued to build the Super Snipe units. The first engine that came out of this collaboration was of 2651cc capacity, developing 118bhp at 5000rpm. This was a square configuration of 82.5mm/3.25in bore and stroke.

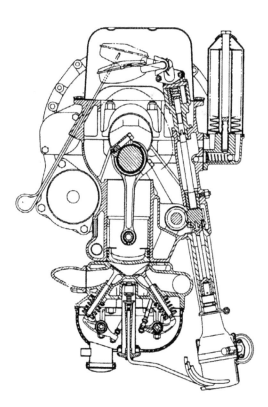

The Armstrong-Siddeley 3.4-litre OHV engine on the left, next to the Series 1 Super Snipe 2.6-litre OHV engine.

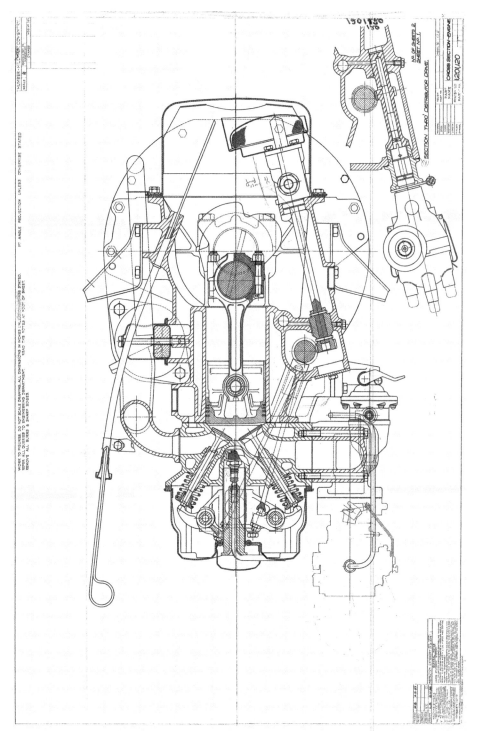

The similarities between the two engines. (Rootes Archive Centre Trust)

The Series 1 Super Snipe made its debut at the London Motor Show in October 1958 retailing at £1,493 for the saloon, £1,643 for the limousine and £1,741 for the estate.

Although sharing the same body as the Hawk, it featured a 'mesh' type grille featuring six horizontal bars and wrap-around chrome sections that attached to the main grille, encompassing the side lights/indicators. It was fitted with drum brakes all round. The manual gearbox was three-speed full synchromesh. Options were power steering, automatic gearbox, overdrive, individual front reclining seats and a radio. Inside, the rear passengers had pull-up picnic tables. There were also rear ashtrays and a cigar lighter (no cigarettes for Humber drivers!). Like the Hawk, it was offered in single-tone and duo-tone colour schemes. Tyres were slightly larger at 670x15 cross ply.

The 8 October 1958 *Motor* magazine reported, 'Both to buy and to run, it is a car that many successful business and professional people will regard as anything but extravagantly expensive, its merits as either a chauffeur-driven or owner-driven car being great, for smooth travel around town or for rapid progress in open country.'

Above: A publicity photograph of the Series 1 Super Snipe.

Right: A close-up of the Series 1 Super Snipe in the styling studio.

The Rootes HQ Devonshire House showroom, showing the new Series 1 Super Snipe saloon and estate. Note the estate has the early arrangement with the number plate and light illumination below the tailgate.

Modifications started soon after full production began.

The Series 2 Super Snipe gained an immediate increase in power by having the engine capacity increased from 2651cc to 2965cc by increasing the bore size from 82.5mm to 87.2mm. The stroke remained the same. A major technical improvement introduced to this model was trailing calliper disc brakes at the front, retaining drum brakes on the rear. This was a Girling system and Rootes had assisted with the systems testing by running gruelling trials with Hawks and prototype Super Snipes and Sunbeam Alpines. The bonnet motif that said 'Humber' on the leading edge of the bonnet on the Series 1 was replaced by individual letters spelling 'HUMBER', in addition to a Snipe bird motif along the centre line of the bonnet.

An unusual version of the Super Snipe could be obtained from the highly respected coachbuilders Harold Radford Ltd of London. Offered as an after-market product, you could have your Super Snipe fitted with a full-length Webasto sunroof, and redesigned reclining front and rear seats that could be fully folded flat to provide two beds and also provide through-loading facility from the boot area. In the boot space, a fold-out picnic table was to one side with tea and coffee making facilities including a kettle and crockery! The centre front seat armrest opened to reveal a mirror, notebook and cigar case. All ideal for Ascot or Goodwood! Having all of this would add around £600 to a car costing £1,475. The conversion package was also available on other cars manufactured by Rolls-Royce, Bentley and Armstrong-Siddeley.

The Metropolitan Police in London took an interest in the new Humbers and had a couple of estates to use as emergency response vehicles. These cars had, in addition to the roof-mounted blue rotating beacon, roof-mounted spotlights and 'Winkworth' bell, heavy-duty suspension as the inside had the rear seat removed and storage unit installed for holding road signs and emergency equipment. There were first-aid boxes, toolboxes, axes, hammers, ropes, bollards, emergency spotlights, and blue lights to highlight blocked roads or to advise drivers to keep clear. Saloons and estate cars could be supplied to suit any local police authority requirements. The Series 2 estate was also one of the first M1 motorway patrol cars, used because of its performance – there were no speed limits in the early days and a car capable of nearly 100mph was a necessity. Motorway patrol cars tended to be white in colour. Interesting to note that any 'luxury' trim was removed from inside the cars, thus the wood door cappings were removed with the doors receiving a new pressing that followed the shape from the padded dashboard crash pad. Rubber flooring replaced the carpet and the glovebox lid was generally removed for installation of the communication equipment. Police specification cars also had a special 'P' letter used as the last of the three-letter vehicle identifier, thus the 'O' for ordinary specified cars was replaced by the 'P' letter. This means genuine police spec cars are easily identified.

Kent's police force also had a fleet of later Series 3 Super Snipe estates for patrolling the new M2 motorway and the Hampshire Constabulary trialled a Super Snipe estate alongside a Volvo 121 estate for similar trunk road emergency use.

The Series 1A Hawk launched in October 1959 and externally was identified by a bodyside flash of an alternate colour that was also used for the roof. The bodyside colour was below the waistband trim with an additional smaller-sized trim to enclose it. Monotone colours were still available. The heater was now standard. Gear ratios were revised together with

A London Metropolitan Police demonstrator Series 2 Super Snipe estate and some of the equipment it carried.

A Series 2 Hawk brochure image.

the gear positions on the steering column gear change, whereby first and second positions were now toward the steering wheel and third and fourth away.

In October 1960, the Series 2 Hawk came along and saw the introduction of disc brakes as per the Super Snipe and larger-sized rear brake drums. Rear suspension (wider leaf springs) and anti-roll bar improvements were also included. On instrumentation, the ammeter, oil pressure gauge and electric screen wash were now standard, having been 'extras' before. The colour schemes were the same, although the two-tone became more subtle with the roof being the alternate colour, which was repeated along the flank of the body but contained within two narrow stainless steel trim strips that now went straight to the rear lights. On the estate cars, a new hinged number plate bracket and lamp unit was mounted on the tailgate below the release button. When the tailgate was pulled down, the number plate would swing down, thus ensuring it was visible with the tailgate open or closed. This feature was included on the Super Snipe estates as well.

In October 1960, four headlamps were introduced on the Series 3 Super Snipe – a first for a British car. These used sealed beam units instead of the normal reflector and bulb lights used up to this point. The outer headlamps had two filaments for dipped and main beam; the inner lamps were main beam only. The front of the car was extended by some 3¾ inches (95mm) forward on the wheel arch and therefore overall length went up from 15 feet 4¾ inches (4.69m) to 15 feet 8 inches (4.77m). There was now a visual difference in appearance between the Hawk and Super Snipe models again. The extension also allowed extra kit, such as air conditioning, to be fitted engine-driven in the engine bay. This change necessitated a grille redesign, now featuring thin horizontal bars across the car incorporating the side and indicator lamps housed in units each side and wrapped around the sides.

The 'HUMBER' letters continued to be used across the leading edge of the bonnet but now, in a nod to safety, the 'Snipe' bird motif was deleted. From the front of the car rearward though, other changes were more subtle – the rest of the car body being the same

The launch of the Series 3 Super Snipe introduced the twin headlamp arrangement at the 1960 London Motor Show.

as before with the exception of the bodyside trim strips that were wider and had a mottled effect pressed into the stainless steel, creating a countersunk cross-section.

Inside, new restyled seats were provided. Standard seating was the bench but with an individual seat option, both options having an armrest. In the back, the rear of the front seat was recessed with the Series 2 car's deep picnic tables replaced by shallower but wider tables with ashtrays and cigar lighter centrally mounted, thus creating an additional 2¼ inches (60mm) of rear knee room. Ventilation was improved by the introduction of air vents at each end of the dashboard, which were opened or closed by a chromed lever. The air was ducted through tubing from the front grille through a repositioned electric ventilation fan, which was moved to the left-hand side of the engine bay to increase space around the engine for maintenance. There were also changes to the front and rear suspension to improve handling.

A Series 3 Super Snipe Kent Police estate.

Six single-tone and five duo-tone paint schemes were offered. For the duo-tone paint scheme, only the roof had the one colour with the rest of the car receiving the other. Metallic paints were introduced at this time.

It cost £1,448 for the basic saloon, £80 extra for the limousine and £300 for the estate. Interestingly, in the USA the prices for a saloon with automatic transmission were $3,995 on the East Coast, and $4,150 on the West Coast. By this time, Rootes had established dealerships throughout the States with primary offices in New York for East Coast and Beverly Hills in California for the West Coast.

Plaudits for the Series 3 Super Snipe were high. The 20 April 1961 *Motoring News* said, 'We should sum up the latest Humber Super Snipe by saying that it is lively in a discreet sort of way, it is lavishly equipped and almost unexpectedly luxurious, it is quiet and restful to drive and it carries with it a prestige label! Anyone who puts one of these in his garage can be said to have arrived!'

Although both the Hawk and Super Snipe were well accepted by the public, the Rootes Group as a whole saw their profits fall. As Geoff Carverhill said in his book *The Rootes Story*, '1959 had seen a pre-tax profit of £3.9 million and an even better figure of £4.4 million in 1960. Compared with BMC who made £26.9 million and Vauxhall £14.1 million the results looked poor but during these few years, Rootes had invested heavily in the Sunbeam Alpine

A Series 3 Super Snipe with the beautiful backdrop of Col des Mosses, Switzerland.

A Series 3 Super Snipe estate. (Rootes Archive Centre Trust)

sports car, the Audax range (Hillman Minx, Singer Gazelle, Sunbeam Rapier) and the Series Humbers so it was a respectable profit margin.' Even so, Rootes were the fourth largest car producer at this time behind Ford, BMC and Vauxhall, holding 10.6 per cent of the market.

Humbers were not known for being involved in rallying, however some did try with not necessarily poor results. Raymond Baxter and co-driver Willy Cave in the 'over 1600cc' class of the 1961 RAC Rally came first driving a Series 3 Super Snipe, helping other Rootes entrants gain a Manufacturer's Team Prize. Three private entry Series 3 Super Snipes were in a rally a little further afield in East Africa in 1962 when one, driven by a Dr Lee Talbot

Above left: Raymond Baxter piloting a Series 3 Super Snipe in the 1961 RAC Rally stage on Brighton seafront.

Above right: Another Series 3 partaking in the 1962 East African Safari.

A Series 3 Super Snipe saloon being assembled from a CKD kit in the Pentone assembly shop of Todd Motors in New Zealand.

and co-driver Mohamed Iqbal, were in contention for a place when they had to retire with suspension issues. Well-known Rootes rally driver Peter Harper and co-driver Ian Hall entered the 1963 British RAC Rally in a Super Snipe but had problems with the gearbox and had to retire.

Company fortunes continued to deteriorate with a strike taking place in 1961 at British Light Steel Pressings in Acton over possible redundancies. BLSP produced the Series Hawk and Super Snipe bodies. This strike lasted thirteen weeks, badly damaging production. Lord Rootes was uncompromising with regard to strikes and would not give in to the workers. Even with this situation, Rootes were developing the Hillman Imp to compete with BMC and the Mini – the Rootes Board being unaware that BMC were losing money on each Mini sold.

The Imp project was further complicated by the fact that Rootes' approach to the Conservative government regarding the expansion of the Ryton-on-Dunsmore facility was turned down as the policy then was to set up new factories in areas of high unemployment. The golden years of Rootes was starting to come to an end.

Car development had to continue and in September 1962 the Series 3 Hawk and Series 4 Super Snipe were launched. The Hawk's fuel tank was enlarged from 12½ gallons to 16 gallons, and it received improved steering gear. Changes to the column gear change reversed the positions with first and second now being next to the steering wheel and third and fourth away. The motif in the centre of the steering wheel changed as well. The rotary controls on the dashboard were removed, with the heating controls of temperature and direction now being sliding levers above the radio position and the lighting now being either side of the retained clock with a two-position switch and a switch for dimming the instrumentation lighting. The body style subtly changed at the rear of the roof, following the angle of the window and not the contour of the upper door frame and gutter. This again followed some of the styling cues of the 210 Series Chevrolets. A stainless steel trim was added to the roof gutter, which went down the new alignment of the back window and along the top of the rear wings. The estates did not have this treatment.

Above left: A Series 3 Hawk brochure image. Note the redesigned rear window and bright trim-to-roof guttering.

Above right: A Series 4 Super Snipe saloon, visually identified by the 'Rootes Group & Snipe Bird' motif in the centre of the radiator grille.

The Super Snipe Series 4 carried over the updates on the Hawk for its launch in October 1962, except that the stainless steel trim on top of the rear wings now met new painted cowls over the top of the rear lights, which in turn had stainless steel-edged trim. New semicircular in cross-section stainless steel bodyside trims now met new chrome strips across the boot lid to the number plate and reversing chrome lamp plinth, which also incorporated the boot release lever and lock – thus making the Super Snipe visually different to the Hawk. On the front grille, a new badge was centrally fitted depicting the Snipe bird motif set against a red background with text below this stating 'Rootes Group'. On the rear saloon doors, the previously fixed quarter-lights were now able to be opened.

Under the bonnet, a new Zenith 42 WIA downdraft carburettor was fitted that boosted engine power output to 124bhp at 5000rpm.

Inside, the dash was largely the same as the Series 3 Hawk but with a few exceptions. The choke control was now a lateral sliding lever – the Hawk was the traditional pull-out knob. The central rotary controls had gone, like the Hawk, but the switches each side of the central clock were now the electric screen wash control and the wipers. Low fuel, low brake fluid and handbrake 'on' indicator lights featured on the dash as well. It now cost £1,542, with this rising by £150 for the limousine and £250 for the estate.

1963 saw a new Humber launched, the Sceptre, which is the subject of chapter 5.

Continuous improvements across the Rootes car range for 1964 saw a redesign to freshen up the look of the Hawk and Super Snipe, Mark 3 Hillman Minx and Singer Vogue with the introduction of a square-shaped roofline. The Sceptre and the estates were not included in this change as being of lower volume the costs would not be justified.

Speaking of costs, the reserves of the Rootes Group were rapidly diminishing and the outlook for survival looked dire. The Chrysler Corporation of America were very keen to enter the UK market and so, much to the regret of Lord Rootes and Sir Reginald Rootes, in 1964 Chrysler acquired 46 per cent of ordinary voting and 65 per cent of non-voting shares in Rootes Motors Ltd in order for the company to survive. Although it allowed Rootes to continue, it marked an end of how Rootes would be able manage itself without interference.

Whether linked to this change or not, Lord Rootes passed away on 12 December 1964. His role on the Rootes Motors Ltd/Chrysler UK board would be taken over by his son Geoffrey Rootes, who inherited the title of Lord Rootes and became Deputy Chairman with Sir Reginald continuing as Chairman. Billy's other son, Brian, became Managing Director of Overseas Operations and Reginald's son Timothy became Managing Director of the UK Passenger Car Division.

In Rootes' styling department in 1963, attention was being paid to what could be done to update the Hawk, but also specifically the Super Snipes within tight financial constraints. Body stylist Peter Leeming's daughter Penny Leeming kept his material, including some sketched preliminary ideas for what could be done to modernise the current Series 4 Super Snipe. His sketches had a new flatter, squarer roof, no uplift of the rear doors, and a swage line above the side trims that went to the rear wings. Effectively the body below the waistline was unchanged, but above it new frames were utilised for the upper part of the doors with the rear fixed quarter-lights now being part of the roofline and not the door. The front and rear windscreens were new and featured new stainless steel inserts. Part of the same collection and photographs of two prototype styling bucks of a next generation Series 5 Super Snipe were taken on the roof of Rootes' development/styling building at the Stoke plant in Humber Road.

The first has the new roofline and redesign of the rear doors to remove the up sweep and move the small fixed window into the roof section. There is evidence of a swage line

Above and below: Series 5 styling bucks on the roof of the Experimental Block at the Stoke plant.

emanating from the top of the rear door and along the rear wing. A complete new front end has been developed, retaining the twin headlamp set-up but encompassed within a new grille assembly. A fold-back at the front of the relatively flat bonnet has the separate letters of H U M B E R. A revised rear end shows what appears to be a narrower tapered boot lid with a new chrome number plate plinth and light incorporating the boot release. The letters H U M B E R are reintroduced as later Series cars used a Snipe bird motif to differentiate between the two models. Restyled new rear lights are seen but it is not clear where the fuel filler cap is. Several versions of overiders are trialled.

The second prototype shows a different bonnet arrangement with a sculptured look, showing similarities to the 1960 Chevrolet Corvair.

Both designs seem to be fairly standard below the waist trim. Due to cost or aesthetics neither prototype progressed, but they do provide an interesting insight into what might have been.

In September 1964, the final redesign of the Series cars was introduced. The only design element passed on from the styling bucks was the new flatter, squarer roofline for both the Series 4 Hawk and Series 5 Super Snipe. It also was used for the Mark 3 Singer Vogue and Hillman Minx. Due to the limited number of estate cars produced, the revised roofline was not incorporated as the cost of re-engineering the roof was deemed uneconomic.

New body colours came in but it marked the end of duo-tone paint schemes as only single colours were available. Fixed rear quarter-lights for the Hawk were part of the roof. Externally, new squared section bumpers were fitted with the overiders receiving rubber inserts. New side/indicator lights were fitted up front below the headlamps and the rear lights were redesigned. Re-profiled stainless steel bodyside trim was fitted. At the rear, a new chrome rear light casting now had individual circular indicator/side and brake and reflector lenses fitted with the offside reflector having the petrol tank cap.

Inside the Series 4 Hawk, new instrumentation was provided featuring red needles to freshen the displays up and new colours for seating, which was now Ambla – an ICI-manufactured plastic with cotton backing. Again, individual reclining seats could be obtained as an option. The door cards also received this material. Overdrive and automatic transmission continued as options. Although radial-ply tyres were now available, Humber stuck to the tried-and-tested tubeless cross-plies, in this case 6.40 x 15. The high-maintenance grease nipples requiring attention every 1,000 miles were also still there, albeit down to twenty-three from twenty-seven due to sealed-for-life track rod ends being fitted.

The Super Snipe also received the new body and detail of the Hawk, becoming the Series 5. The lower body remained the same as the Series 4 but received the new bumpers and lost the trim across the boot lid. The fixed rear quarter-lights of the Hawk, which were part of the roof, were now able to be opened for ventilation. There was an increase in engine power with the introduction of a new inlet manifold to mount two Stromberg CD-175 carburettors. This helped increase power output to a gross 137.5bhp at 5000rpm, up from the previous 124bhp on the Series 4. Additional exhaust silencers were also fitted to the redesigned exhaust system. The options of automatic transmission using the Borg-Warner DG box, three-speed manual, or manual with Laycock overdrive were available. An alternator was used – a Lucas 10AC type with separate regulator giving a higher current output at lower engine speed. Power steering was standard. The front anti-roll bar was increased in diameter and a new rear anti-roll bar fitted with new rear

Above: The Series 4 Hawk.

Left: The Series 5 Super Snipe.

FOR THE MAN WITH DRIVING AMBITION

to get ahead

You don't know his face, but there's purpose written on it. At a little over 30 he's the youngest director on the board; a top-level man with a gift for getting the right decisions out of his clients. And he drives a new Humber Super Snipe. He chose it for its perfection in power and luxury. The big, 3-litre engine immediately responsive to his touch, silently powerful, with vivid acceleration to 100 mph... the spacious interior, luxuriously upholstered in real English hide, appointed with walnut veneer and thickly carpeted...the firm, smooth ride to cushion along a crotchety client or soothe away the miles on long Continental holidays. Ask your secretary to arrange for you a test-drive of the superb new Humber Super Snipe. Smooth 6-cylinder, 3-litre engine; power-assisted steering; front disc brakes. Overdrive or fully automatic transmission and whitewall tyres available as extras. *£1,511.19.7 inc £261.19.7 p.t. Also available **New Humber Hawk.** Elegantly restyled; improved gearbox, steering, suspension, *£1,095.2.1 inc £190.2.1 p.t. *All prices ex-works.

HUMBER SUPER SNIPE

 ROOTES MOTORS LIMITED
LONDON SHOWROOMS AND EXPORT DIVISION ROOTES LIMITED DEVONSHIRE HOUSE PICCADILLY LONDON W1

The Series 5 Imperial.

dual-rate springs to improve road holding. As with the Hawk, cross-ply tyres were retained, 6.70x15 using the Dunlop RS5 high performance tyre.

A new model was brought in to sit above the Super Snipe and would see a name last used in 1954 resurrected – Imperial.

Competition in the medium luxury car 'wood and leather' market was quite intense in early 1960s. BMC had the Vanden Plas 3 Litre, soon to be upgraded to the 4-litre 'R' by using the military division Rolls-Royce B60 6-cylinder engine. Rover had their Mark 3 P5 model and Jaguar the Mk2 saloon. Thus, to move the Super Snipe up a level some further enhancements needed to be added to the standard Super Snipe specification.

Launching in October 1964, the Imperial was fitted out by Rootes coachbuilders Thrupp & Maberly in Humber Road, Cricklewood, with the following features added as standard:

- Black vinyl Everflex roof covering.
- 'IMPERIAL' script on front doors and Snipe bird motif on boot lid, changing to 'IMPERIAL' later.
- Red warning lights on door edges, which illuminated when doors were opened.
- West of England cloth seat coverings with leather as an option.
- West of England cloth headlining as standard.
- Individual front reclining Reutter seats with armrests and, fitted to the rear of the seat, drop-down walnut-veneered trinket trays for the rear passengers.
- Armstrong-developed 'Selectaride' rear shock absorbers giving four options of ride comfort from 'soft' to 'hard', selected by a rotary switch mounted below the right-hand side dash.

- A built-in rug for the rear floor on top of the existing deep pile carpet.
- Pull-down reading lights and hand straps for rear passengers.
- Rear compartment heating with vent grilles in the seat base plus driver-operated control to direct air onto the rear window for demisting.
- Radiomobile radio as standard with front and rear speakers and a driver control for adjusting sound balance between the front and rear compartments.
- Badge bar with 'Rootes' fog and spot lamps.
- Step sill cover inserts saying 'Thrupp & Maberly, London'.
- The Limousine option was available with cloth on the rear seats and leather up front with a glass division.
- Automatic transmission only – a Borg-Warner DG type initially, and type 35 later. No manual option.

It is interesting to note how many journeys the car had made prior to being sold. BLSP in Acton built the body, which then was transhipped to Thrupp & Maberly in Cricklewood for painting, glazing and trimming before being transported to Ryton-on-Dunsmore for fitting the engine, transmission, front and rear suspension and final testing before being despatched to dealerships around the country.

The Imperial at the 1964 Motor Show launch, with Raymond Baxter doing a piece to camera.

Above and right: At Thrupp & Maberly, finishing the interior and undertaking final inspection of the Imperial prior to the body going to Ryton for final assembly. (Richard Langworth)

The Imperial retailed at £1,794 including purchase tax. This was some £200 more than the standard Series 5 Super Snipe. This was still very good value in this sector of the market as the competition were more expensive – the Mk3 Rover 3-litre was £1,858, the Jaguar 3.8S was £1,885, and the new Vanden Plas Princess 4-litre was £1,995. The main overseas competitor was generally seen to be the Mercedes-Benz 220 saloon, priced at £2,278.

The motoring press were generally impressed and the well-respected Bill Boddy wrote in a road test for *Motor Sport*, 'This is outwardly a substantial looking car but by no means excessively bulky. It is impressive in rather an old-fashioned subtle way, like a Rolls-Royce, and it is certainly extremely well appointed and equipped, so that even the most demanding and fastidious purchasers could scarcely complain.'

Other car manufacturers also decided to upgrade some of their models in a similar fashion. In 1965 Ford had a special edition Mk3 Zodiac, the Executive. This had leather-faced seats and wood-effect dashboard, plus other extras. Rover had the Mk3 3-litre with an upgraded interior and even Vauxhall got in on the act in 1966 with their large car, the PC type Cresta. The Viscount was introduced fitted with leather seating and individual front reclining seats, an Everflex vinyl roof covering, wood-effect dashboard, power steering and electrically operated windows. It had the venerable 3.3-litre straight-six engine mated to a two-speed automatic transmission and a revised grille arrangement, making the car look different to the standard Cresta.

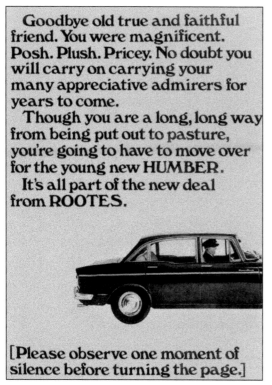

Above left and above right: Advertising the end of the large Humbers and introduction of the Mk3 Sceptre.

The Australian Chrysler Valiant was offered in the UK as the Series car replacement.

In 1965, the Super Snipe was upgraded to Series 5A by fitting the improved Borg-Warner-type 35 automatic gearbox where this option was specified. The change was visually apparent to the driver as on the gear position quadrant atop the steering column cowl the 'Drive' position was now 'D1' and 'D2'. In 'D1' the car would start away in first gear, whereas in 'D2' it would start in second gear if a brisk acceleration from standstill was not required.

However, the age of the big Humbers – the Hawk, Super Snipe and the Imperial – was declining and Chrysler's control was starting to impinge on day-to-day running of the Rootes Group and its investment in new models. Super Snipe and Imperial production ceased in June 1967 with Hawk saloons finishing in October. Estate variants ended in January 1968. Chrysler offered the Australian-built Valiant to fill the gap but it was not a success. So, was that it as far as development was concerned of the Super Snipe and Imperial? Well, not quite... as we shall see.

4

The Series V8 Programme and Beyond

The Sunbeam arm of Rootes had introduced a neatly designed new sports car in 1959 – the Alpine, a two-door open sports car. This was designed by Ken Howes and was aimed to sell at under £1,000. It was powered initially by the 1494cc 4-cylinder Hillman Minx engine, giving reasonable performance. The prototype and early cars were produced in partnership with Armstrong-Siddeley in Coventry, who had spare manufacturing capacity at their Burlington Works. As we saw with the early Series 1 Super Snipe engine, Armstrong-Siddeley had a good working relationship with Rootes. The car was a great success with the advanced clean line design it had.

However, in the American market the car was underpowered in comparison with other cars in the sports car sector such the Ford Mustang and Chevrolet Corvette. In the US, V8 engines were considered the norm.

Norman Garrad was Rootes Competition Manager, responsible for some great rally wins for Sunbeam-Talbot and Sunbeam Rapier cars in the 1950s and 1960s. His son, Ian, was Rootes' West Coast representative based in California. He tentatively approached Carroll Shelby, the well-known and respected tuning expert on the West Coast, about sourcing a V8 engine suitable to install in the narrow confines of the Alpine engine bay. Ian Garrad was acutely aware of how the Rootes family board might view what he was trying to do and thus kept his plans well under cover. Conveniently, a meeting in February 1963 with Brian Rootes, Rootes' Export Manager, when he was attending a West Coast Rootes dealer seminar, gave the opportunity to broach the subject directly with a member of the Rootes Board. Brian was surprisingly keen and gave encouragement to Ian to progress his idea as he could see the potential of a V8 engine for the Alpine. Several meetings with Carroll Shelby brought about ideas on what engine might be suitable for installation in the Alpine's engine bay and eventually a narrow block Ford engine was selected.

With prototype work done, a 4.2-litre Ford engine was found to be the best option to be installed. The car was accepted by Lord Rootes and the Rootes Board and it went into production as the Sunbeam Tiger. The car launched in 1965.

It came as no surprise that other Rootes cars were considered for V8 engine installation and the Super Snipe was top of the list. However, the big problem was that the Tiger used a Ford engine, which did not sit well with Rootes' new partners, Chrysler. Work was therefore commissioned to see what Chrysler V8 units might be suitable for the much larger and more generous Humber engine bay.

Other manufacturers were also looking at using V8 engines. Rover had started to dabble with the all-aluminium lightweight American Buick '215' type V8 engine that would go on to be used extensively throughout their range of cars and Land Rovers. Daimler was already using the Edward Turner-designed 4.5-litre V8 for their Daimler Majestic and the 2.5-litre version for the Mk2 Daimler 250 saloon.

Work commenced in 1964 at the Rootes Vehicle Development Department in the Stoke plant. The programme was to be known internally as the Snipe Chrysler project. The intention was that the V8 would be offered as an upgrade to the standard Super Snipe and Imperial.

The first vehicle to be experimented with was a Mk1 Humber Sceptre fitted with a 4.4-litre, 190bhp, 4-barrel Holley carburettor Chrysler engine coupled to an automatic gearbox. On the banked test circuits at the Motor Industry Research Association (MIRA) facilities near Nuneaton, it achieved a top speed of over 130mph and a 0–60 time of 9.1 seconds – the standard Sceptre had managed 17.1 seconds. Performance was not far from that of the Sunbeam Tiger. As far as can be determined, the Sceptre was kept at the development unit at Stoke for a number of years and used as a general development car before, sadly, being broken up.

A project plan was produced on 18 August 1965, detailing proposals involving the use of six prototype and six pre-production Super Snipes. Each prototype car was classified as 'SC' (Snipe Chrysler) and SC1, a silver-grey Series 5A saloon, was fitted with a Chrysler 312 CI 250bhp, 4-barrel Holley carburettor V8 engine and a three-speed manual gearbox. A Salisbury differential was installed within a Chrysler axle to cope with the torque, with the original Humber Super Snipe wheel hubs welded onto the half-shafts so that standard wheels could be fitted. The engine and transmission had to be installed from above the engine bay as intrusions in the bay meant that installation from underneath, the way the standard 6-cylinder engine was installed on the line, could not be achieved. New engine mounts also had to be designed to mount the engine on the front suspension cross-member. As the engines had automatic chokes, the sliding choke control on the dashboard was removed. It went to MIRA and performed spectacularly, achieving around 125mph – in four laps it had wrecked the standard Dunlop RS5 cross-ply tyres!

Returning to Humber Road, SC1 had its engine changed for a less powerful 273 CI V8 and a 2-barrel carburettor for further testing. This only developed 150bhp, which was barely more powerful than the now standard 2965cc straight six with the twin Stromberg carburettors. However, due to the V8 engines having been built with improved casting techniques, there was a weight saving of some 50lbs (22.7kgs). SC2 and SC3 were fitted with 273 CI 4.4-litre V8s with 10.5 to 1 compression ratios, giving an output of 218bhp at 5200rpm. The main problem the engineers found was that the fuel lines from the rear tank and brake lines had to be realigned to avoid the twin exhaust system. The radiator needed upgrading and a new seven-bladed fan fitted. A transmission cooling radiator had to be provided, and the brake servo unit required pushing up into the nearside inner wing. A special narrow 12-volt battery was used to maximise the width of the bay to give sufficient clearance around the engine.

SC3 was a left-hand drive Super Snipe, SC5 an Imperial and SC6 another Super Snipe. A list of additional items to be added to V8 car's specification was proposed, including electric windows, an early Lucas cruise control system, intermittent speed control

The SC1 interior, showing manual gear change and a rev counter.

screen wipers, automatically dipping rear view mirror and air conditioning. Quite a luxury package!

However, technical issues such as burnt piston crowns and blown head gaskets affected the cars with the higher-tuned engines. The engines required 100 octane petrol, which was not always available at garages and was more expensive. Adding to the list of issues, fuel consumption was worse than the standard 6-cylinder engine.

As Geoff Carverhill says in his book *The Rootes Story*, in early 1964 Chrysler had already, prior to Lord Rootes's death, obtained 46 per cent of Rootes ordinary voting shares and 65 per cent of non-voting shares – meaning they were increasing their control of the Rootes Board. In January 1965, the Rootes Board was revamped with Sir Reginald Rootes becoming Chairman, with Geoffrey as Deputy Chairman and Head of Rootes Motors Ltd. Rootes was then split into three groups. Brian Rootes, Sir Reginald's son, became Chairman of the Overseas and Home Distribution Division; Timothy Rootes was Managing Director of the Passenger Car Division; and Rex Watson-Lee held the position of Manging Director of Commer-Karrier in Dunstable. In April 1967, Chrysler took full control of the Rootes Board after receiving Labour government approval from Sir Anthony Wedgwood Benn, then Minister of Technology. It is interesting to note that the Prime Minister, Harold Wilson, was a fan of Humber cars and had access to one when touring the country on official business.

A major programme of rationalisation followed, but also a much-needed cash injection of £17 million from Chrysler. Sir Reginald Rootes, who had taken over as Chairman from his brother Billy, retired and enjoyed ten years of retirement before he passed away. The sons of Billy and Reggie would carry on in key parts of the new management structure.

An immediate visual indication of the new owners of Rootes appeared on cars, vans and trucks with the addition of Chrysler's five-pointed Pentastar badging. This was applied to vehicles and featured prominently on brochures and advertisements.

Chrysler also stopped production of the Hawk, Super Snipe and Imperial, thus bringing to an end the large car range. The Sceptre Mk3 model would carry on until 1976. Stocks of the three models were sold off by dealers with generous discounts. New adverts in car magazines pushed the Sceptre model and sometimes denigrated the large cars as being out of date – by then, they were.

As Chrysler could see no point in further developing a ten-year-old car, the V8 programme was stopped, though other proposals were still being considered. As an interim measure, Chrysler promoted the Australian-built V8-powered Valiant four-door saloon and produced promotions to offer this to the existing Humber cliental. But the cars had no wood or leather and sales dived; it was never accepted by the traditional Humber buyer as being a true replacement and after two years was quietly dropped.

Above and right: An SC4 nears the end of its restoration, with its 'V8' badges fitted and bodyshell close to completion. (Keith Bagnall)

We do know a little about what happened to the V8 prototypes. Brian Rootes, brother of Geoffrey Rootes, owned a second Imperial V8 that was part of the prototype run and registered GDU 495D, but it's assumed to have been destroyed after his ownership.

Fortunately, two of these extremely rare cars do survive. SC4, a silver Super Snipe, Coventry-registered EHP 622C, is emerging from a full restoration by Club member Keith Bagnall. The car was rescued in 1982 in poor condition by a then Club member who restored it but almost turned it into a custom car, complete with Wolfrace wheels. It then went to the USA before returning to the UK to for another extensive restoration bringing it back to almost original specification.

The second restored car is SC5, the April 1966 maroon Imperial Coventry-registered as GDU 492D. Following the cancellation of the project, it became the personal car of Sir Reginald Rootes in his retirement and was registered to him in March 1968. This car had the 273 CI 4.4-litre engine with the 2-barrel Holley carburettor producing around 150bhp driving through a Torqueflite automatic gearbox. It was sold on in 1973 and passed to a private owner in Ashford, Kent, who owned it for a number of years. However, it deteriorated badly and passed to a Club member for and eventually to Denis Cunningham and his son Darren, who carried out a thorough rebuild. The car is now on display at the marvellous Isle of Man Motor Museum.

According to Graham Robson's *Cars of the Rootes Group*, losses for Rootes for 1966/7 amounted to some £10.8 million. However, development work still had to continue for the Hawk/Super Snipe/Imperial replacements and the story now turns to look at proposals for a new generation of large Humber to sit above the Sceptre.

Above left and above right: SC5 is now on display in the IOM Museum following its major rebuild.

Going back to 1963, the Rootes Design and Development team were developing a new design known internally as the 'B' car. With the injection of new capital from Chrysler, a brand-new design facility was established at Whitley, just south of Coventry city centre, with all the existing design team transferring from Humber Road. The 'B' car would eventually become the 'Avenger' model, designed by Roy Axe and his team. This proved to be a winner in the last years under Rootes management prior to Chrysler taking full control. Alongside the Avenger 'B' car, there was also a 'C' car put forward for consideration with a larger version of the Avenger body, designed by the same styling team. This was to become the next generation large Humber, complete with a new engine.

The early plan for this car was to have two versions, the Sceptre and the Snipe. The former was to be powered by the existing 1725cc 4-cylinder engine used throughout the Rootes vehicle range, and the Snipe would have received a brand-new engine being developed in-house – a V6! It is believed that there were going to be two engines, a 2.0-litre and a 2.5-litre. Both were 60-degree V6s.

By 1970, with a budget of about £35 million, around £31 million had been spent on all the machine and production tooling. Production started building prototype engines and putting them into development cars, including a couple of Avengers and Series 4 Hawks, for running trials. There were also plans afoot to fit De-Dion rear axles and five-speed manual gearboxes as well as automatics. However, Chrysler's involvement proved a sticking point – as part of their strategy for Europe, they had also purchased Simca of France and Barreiros of Spain, who built cars and trucks.

I am indebted to Tim Cunningham for sharing his late father John's anecdotes of testing a 'C' car prototype at Bruntingthorpe airfield north-east of Coventry. Bruntingthorpe airfield was interesting as, after it closed as an operational RAF airbase, Rootes stepped in to buy it in 1972 as a proving ground. Prior to moving to Bruntingthorpe his father remembered that Wellesbourne airfield in Warwickshire, not far from Gaydon, was also used by Rootes for this purpose from 1967.

This car, ALN 913H registered in August 1969, was fitted with 2.5-litre V6 engine and was undergoing arduous testing by John. It was fitted with electric windows and quality seating. Tim remembers his father John saying that he thought the car cost around £30,000 to build in 1969 – a not inconsiderable amount of money.

However, across the Channel, Simca were also developing a new design of large saloon, code number 929, with a new range of engines. The last thing Chrysler wanted was two of their acquired companies trying to compete for the same segment of the market, so one had to be dropped. There followed a year or so of fraught negotiations between the three companies (Chrysler, Rootes, Simca) with deep concern in Coventry over the decision Chrysler might take, which spurred one employee to write the following brilliant ditty in the *Coventry Evening Telegraph*, based on a hymn by William Whiting, 'For Those in Peril on the Sea'. It was seen by the author in Graham Robson's book *Cars of the Rootes Group*.

Lord God Chrysler from afar,
Said we'll build a motor-car,
To follow 'Arrow' and the 'B',
Until its born, we'll call it 'C',
We'll raise a super power train crew,

And use some new procedures too,
We'll pay a little over par,
And adorn it with the 'Pentastar',
The game is played to Chrysler's rules,
Machines aplenty and all the tools,
Until at last there dawns a day,
And doubt arises, will it pay?,
Rumour says the project's dead,
The future's viewed with obvious dread;
Lord God Chrysler pray for me,
And those in peril on the 'C'.

In 1970, a high-level meeting was held with both Rootes and Simca design teams presenting their proposals for this new car range to the Chrysler Board.

The decision taken by Chrysler was not positive for Rootes and although UK prototype cars were running, even complete with new 'Sceptre' badging, it was all in vain as the decision taken was to use the UK base car design but build the car in the Poissy plant of Simca, just outside of Paris. It was also decided to use the existing 1812cc 4-cylinder Simca engine.

The car became the Chrysler 180, with the Simca 929 project dropped. The French also had design control of the interior and thus the UK's preferred walnut veneers, leather seating, air conditioning, electric windows and other luxury appointments were thrown out for the French-inspired plastic wood effect and large 1970s velour seats. The interior was pretty much brown everywhere. It was a bitter disappointment for the British team and effectively marked the end of Rootes as a design entity.

Tim Cunningham's father, John, thought that a large quantity of crated V6 engines that had been produced and in storage at Bruntingthorpe were destroyed when the 'C' project collapsed. An appalling shame.

The Chrysler 180 launched to a largely underwhelmed buying public and motoring press.

It was later joined by a 2-litre variant, unsurprisingly called the Chrysler 2-litre, complete with a vinyl roof covering, fog and spot lights, additional luxury features and automatic transmission as standard. Both cars continued to be built in France and also by Barreiros in Spain, soon to become Chrysler-Spain, with later other engine variants. Although a reasonable success in greater Europe, it certainly was not in the UK.

There was yet another intriguing story of a proposal for a new Super Snipe and this involved collaboration with a local motor manufacturer who Rootes had helped previously by using their facilities – Jensen Motors of West Bromwich. The following information came from Keith Anderson of the Jensen Owners Club and was published in our Club magazine.

Jensen had built for Rootes 7,067 examples of the Sunbeam Tiger from 1964, as Rootes had insufficient space at Ryton to assembly the car. Although building their own luxury sports car, the Jensen Interceptor, they were also assembling for Volvo the P1800 using bodies supplied from Pressed Steel in Linwood opposite the Imp plant. Later, the Pressed Steel factory would be sold to Rootes/Chrysler with the combined factories being renamed 'Rootes Scotland Ltd'.

The Chrysler 2-Litre.
Think of it as your favourite armchair.

The Chrysler 2-Litre will give you one of the most comfortable and satisfying drives you've ever had.

From the rich velour cloth seats, to its smooth Torque-Flite automatic transmission, the 2-Litre is built to take the strain out of even the most taxing drives.

If, however, you'd prefer a manual gearbox without sacrificing any of your comfort, look no farther than the Chrysler 180.

Apart from the gearbox, a slightly smaller engine and a small difference in interior trim, it's identical to the 2-Litre.

The same high level of specification, including inertia reel seat belts, servo-assisted brakes.

Economy: up to 31mpg.*

Top speed of around 106 mph; more than enough for today's needs.

Electronic ignition: instant starting in even the coldest or wettest weather.

The unique Chrysler protection of The Protector.

And, of course, that same feeling of well-being you always get when you settle down in your favourite armchair.

Chrysler

Taking better care of you and your car.

*Manufacturer's figures achieved at an average speed of 36mph over a course of 80 miles of town and country driving conditions.

CHRYSLER
UNITED KINGDOM

An advert for the Chrysler 2-litre.

Chrysler's takeover of Rootes raised the issue of their dislike of a Rootes car using a Ford engine and so, in 1967, the contract with Jensen building the Sunbeam Tiger was terminated. However, the Rootes/Chrysler Board, alongside the internal 'C' project, wanted to see if an outside manufacturer could provide a better-costed quotation to build a complete car compared to it being done in-house. A proposal was sent to the Jensen Board.

They were commissioned by Rootes/Chrysler with instructions to 'Examine all major aspects related to the possible production of a large four-door saloon car [for Super Snipe and Imperial cars] in terms of design, production feasibility and cost, against guidelines set out by Product Planning department, Passenger Car Division, Rootes Motors Ltd. Guideline costing, £1,150 for the Super Snipe and £1,375 for the Imperial car.'

The proposal was sent to Jensen on 22 August 1967. Jensen brought in the Vignale Design Studio in Italy and local Coventry company Motor Panels for their input to the proposal. The Rootes Design brief was that the car would have the following features:

- Chrysler 273 CI or 318 CI in V8 engine.
- Torqueflite automatic gearbox.
- Fully adjustable steering column.
- Dual-circuit disc braking.
- Through-flow ventilation/air conditioning.
- Leather seating.
- Electric windows.
- Variable-speed wipers.
- Selectaride dampers at the rear.
- Limited slip differential.
- Numerous additional driver and passenger comfort amenities.

Jensen went to work immediately. As their Interceptor model utilised a strong tubular chassis, this was considered a satisfactory base for the planned Humber. By December 1967 Jensen Motors had responded, delivering to Rootes the design proposal, which included prepared key drawings and a fully costed proposal. They detailed seventy-nine panels that would need producing.

The car would have a finished length of 190 inches (4.83m) compared with the standard Super Snipe of 188 inches (4.78m). The width was 72 inches (2.0m) compared with 69.5 inches (1.76m) and the height was 58 inches (1.46m) compared with 61 inches (1.55m). This meant a slightly lower and sleeker design.

For the Super Snipe, Jensen quoted a wholesale price to Rootes of £1,300 and £1,475 for the Imperial based on production of 1,500 units over a three-year period. This compared with current retail prices for the Series 5A Super Snipe of £1,590 and Imperial of £1,925. It also provided Jensen a modest profit of £118 per car. The Super Snipe costing was greater than what Rootes hoped and so was discontinued; however costing of the Imperial was deemed feasible and so Jensen Motors continued their work to fully develop the design for the Imperial. But despite a very comprehensive response from Jensen this project was eventually turned down by Chrysler, who were now fully in control at Rootes. It was a blow for Jensen who, although starting to enjoy a renaissance with the Interceptor, could have done with the extra work. It is interesting to note that the proposed Imperial costing £1,475 and probably selling in the region of £2,200 would have been very similar to a four-door version of the Interceptor. Jensen sold their Interceptor for £3,743, with build cost much the same! It is thought that the design would have looked something like the Roll-Royce Silver Shadow coming onto the market in 1965.

In 1967, Chrysler instigated major rationalisation in the business in order to save costs. With the large Humbers gone, British Light Steel Pressings together with the Thrupp & Maberly factory in London were both closed as their work could be absorbed into the Coventry factories. Pressed Steel at Linwood was now under Rootes ownership as a panel producer.

So, was that was the end for the large Humbers? Not quite.

In April 1987, *Autocar* magazine ran a news item. A former marketing manager of the post-Chrysler (by then Peugeot-Talbot) plant at Linwood produced his ambitious plans for a new generation Humber. Andrew Boulton had been working on plans to fill a hole he saw in the 1980s luxury car market. He was a marketing specialist for Chrysler (UK) from 1976 to 1981 when he left to concentrate on developing his plans to create an individual motor company – no mean feat for an individual.

To say his plans were ambitious was an understatement. He wanted to produce two new cars, developed by outside specialists, and call them Humbers purely to ensure the name placed his new design of luxury car in the right area of the market. The company name was to be the Humber Motor Company Ltd and would have no connection at all with Rootes/Chrysler Humbers.

On 27 March 1987, he released this statement to the press:

I have thoroughly researched the [luxury car] market and I think that executive and luxury car manufacture is the most profitable sector and that's where I want Humber to be.

Humber cars used to be compared with some of the best in the world in road tests and the name has escaped the problems that have plagued other quality manufacturers in the last decade.

Initially I would want two models, a 2.7 litre executive car and a 5.4 litre V12 luxury car which could be designed by specialists such as Giugiaro and Porsche and be ready to go into production in five years.

The engines quoted were to be sourced from Rover for the KV6 2.7-litre V6 Honda-derived engine and the V12 from Jaguar.

Boulton envisaged taking over the old Bathgate British Leyland truck plant to produce the cars.

However, he faced an uphill battle. He needed to raise £100,000 just for the business plan to present to investors and, at this early stage, there were not many. British Leyland were unwilling to enter negotiations for the Bathgate site as they saw no real chance of him ever raising sufficient finance to complete a purchase.

Not to be deterred, Andrew Boulton continued his crusade to attract investors and commenced further briefs to the local and national motoring press.

On 2 April 1987, he stated in a further brief,

It is anticipated that an initial manufacturing labour force of 2,000 will be required to produce the start-up volume of 10,000 vehicles per year.

It is intended that the facility will be structured to break-even on a single shift capacity of 60,000 vehicles per year. Thus eventually, as many as 10,000 jobs could be created when the annual output hits 200,000 cars and would put the firm on a comparable footing with Saab, BMW and Volvo.

It was thought that as much as £500 million could be required to obtain the premises, equip the plant, design the cars and have all the tooling, parts and labour to actually produce the cars.

The project would appear to have been doomed from the start as East Lothian District Council were planning to develop Bathgate into a 'megastore' site, which financially was more viable than Boulton's plans.

He was also still to negotiate with Peugeot-Talbot about using the 'Humber' name.

The crucial issue of whether the buying public would purchase the cars was also something that needed serious consideration. To some, 'Humber' as a name may mean a car that did not break any technical barriers and was generally dowdy and unexciting. Was this the right image for the target customers? Perhaps not. Companies in this sector of the market such as Mercedes-Benz, BMW, and Jaguar Land Rover spent millions in developing new car designs so a 'start-up' company such as Boulton's 'Humbers' would have needed high levels of financial support from banks and backers to get the project off the ground.

Not surprisingly, the project folded two years later.

5

The Sceptres

A brand-new Humber entered the market in 1963 – the Sceptre.

The origins of this car can be found in a new concept within the car industry – badge engineering.

In order to save costs, a basic design could be developed into a family of cars to suit specific markets. Examples of this could be found in America with General Motors and Ford developing common models, and BMC with Pininfarina of Italy-designed cars being badged as Austin Cambridge, Morris Oxford or MG Magnettes.

In his book *The Rootes Story*, Geoff Carverhill says in 1953 Rootes approached their design partner the Loewy Design Studio in London to assist in developing a new range of cars, all to be based on a common floorpan. This was to become the 'Audax' range. The first car to benefit from this new design was the Series 1 Sunbeam Rapier, a very smart two-door coupé launched at the October 1955 London Motor Show. Its design was similar in some respects to the Studebaker Starliner in the US, also styled by Loewy. The Rapier featured a wrap-around rear window with a pillarless design on the two-door body. Together with eye-catching bright two-tone colour schemes, it was a stunning car to be launched in a rather drab Britain at that time.

The floorpan was then used as the base for the new Hillman Minx Series 1 in May 1956, followed in September by an all-new Singer Gazelle Mk1. This was the first Singer to be produced by Rootes following their takeover of the ailing company.

In 1961, product planning, under Ted White, was given the brief to develop an Audax replacement for Hillman and Sunbeam. The Hillman version would become the Super Minx Mk1 with the original Audax range Minx and Gazelle cars dropped.

The revamp was completed with the Mk1 Hillman Super Minx coming to the market in October 1962. The decision was taken to keep the Audax range cars, which comprised the standard Minx, Husky, Singer Gazelle, Sunbeam Rapier, Alpine and Tiger, but to merely update the existing designs. The company pressed ahead with new models based on the Super Minx.

With the Mk1 Super Minx now complete, attention turned to the Sunbeam saloon – to become the Mk4 Rapier, following on from the Mk3A. The usual development work of making clay models and the building of a 'mock-up' of the Rapier Mk4 followed. The engine would be the tried-and-tested 1592cc 4-cylinder engine developing 80bhp using twin Zenith carburettors, the same combination fitted to the Series 2 Alpine. Work continued preparing for a launch in 1963.

Above, below and opposite: Prototype pictures of the embryonic Mk4 Rapier outside the Experimental Shop. RAPIER badging was fitted to doors and wings as appropriate.

At least three prototypes were built for testing and were given the test vehicle references of RAP 1, RAP 2 and RAP 3.

Rover had been working on an advanced 'executive' saloon for a number of years that would bring in many advanced engineering features – even trialling a gas turbine power unit. It was scheduled to be released to the public in the autumn of 1963 as the 'P6' Rover 2000. Its advanced features were a new overhead camshaft, 4-cylinder 1978cc engine, and a unique body structure 'skeleton' with all panels, including the roof, bolted to it. With a rakish body design it was no wonder it was universally acclaimed when launched and awarded the European Car of the Year accolade for 1963.

This may have been the reason Rootes decided to launch the car as a Humber instead of a Sunbeam as planned, as from a Rootes perspective it would make sense to have its new Humber model launched ahead of the Rover into this executive sector of the market.

The Mk1 Sceptre, built in the Ryton factory, was released in January 1963 ahead of the Rover that launched on 9 October. The new Sceptre had an impressive specification including a first in having a double-curvature high-level windscreen developed by Triplex. It also had a wrap-around rear window slightly hooded by the roofline, twin headlamps similar to the Series 3 Super Snipe, front servo-assisted disc brakes, individual front seats with multi-adjustment, and a four-speed gearbox with synchromesh on second, third and fourth with overdrive standard on third and fourth. Automatic transmission was not offered.

Inside, the car had a sports car-style comprehensive instrumentation including a rev counter with the complete dash in black, full carpeting, and individual reclining front seats. Outside, there were twin headlamps, reversing lights, opening quarter-lights front and rear and greasing points were eliminated (the Series cars retained twenty-three greasing points

An early production Mk1 Sceptre stands in the Ryton factory.

until the end of production). The fuel tank, rather than being in the usual under-boot floor position, was incorporated within the rear nearside wing in the boot area with the filler cap on top of the wing by the rear window. It was available in four single-tone and five duo-tone colour schemes. The only options available for this model were seat belts, radio and whitewall tyres. The Sceptre retailed at just over £997.

The MK1 Sceptre brochure. Some detailing was obviously still not right; painted headlamp 'eyebrows' are seen here, whereas production cars were chrome.

It had a top speed of 90mph with a respectable 0–60 time of 17.2 seconds. From its launch, it was a great success with over 17,000 cars produced.

As expected with any new model, modifications soon followed and in 1964 synchromesh became available on first gear. A single compound twin-choke Solex carburettor replaced the two Zenith carburettors, which helped to raise power output from 80 to 84bhp. The colour schemes were revised with six single-tones and only three duo-tones and rubber-faced overiders were fitted. Although estate bodies were available with the Minx and Singer, the Sceptre was not offered with this body style.

The NEW

HUMBER 90 DE LUXE SALOON

Above and right: These Australian market brochures show UK market Hillman Super Minxes and Mk 3 Singer Vogues as the 'Humber 90' and 'Humber Vogue' respectively!

THE NEW Humber Vogue

The Sceptre was exported around the world either fully built or CKD (Completely Knocked Down). Primary markets were Australia, New Zealand, Ireland and South Africa.

The practice of restricted imports continued into the 1960s in Australia and New Zealand with some Series 3 Minx cars becoming the Humber 80 and the Mk1 Super Minx becoming the Humber 90. In 1964, the Mk3 Singer Vogue became the Humber Vogue with its UK-derived sales brochure carefully obscuring the SINGER name on the grille!

An unusual diversion also occurred in 1963 involving the Italian coachbuilders Carrozzeria Touring of Milan. This company was known for designing the Aston Martin DB4, 5 and 6; Ferraris; Alfa-Romeos; and other prestige cars using a unique production process to construct the body using a steel tubular frame with panels attached. The company patented this production method as 'Superleggera', though a conventional steel chassis or floorpan was still required.

The Series 1 Sunbeam Alpine was presented to the public in 1959. Part of the launch programme was to have the car taken down to the south of France for the motoring press to see and test drive. Alec Caine was chosen to be the Rootes engineer to look after the Alpine launch in Cannes in July, which went very well.

He later took an Alpine to the Turin Salon in October of that same year and spoke to a Touring representative at the show. Alec told them of a few design issues that had not yet been resolved, such as the clutch and brake pedal positioning, and asked if they could help. They did, and the modification they carried out was fitted on the UK assembly line at Armstrong Siddeley's plant in Coventry. Such a strong bond was created between the two companies that in 1961 a contract was signed with Rootes to commence assembling Hillman Super Minxes, Sunbeam Alpines and Humber Sceptres from CKD kits sent from Coventry. The local Rootes agent in Milan was managed by George Carless. With the clientele he sold Rootes cars to, he thought that a sporting saloon could prove to be successful. He privately approached Touring, who were quite receptive to the idea. They developed some sketches and proposals and sent them to Brian Rootes in Coventry with a request to build a prototype. Brian gave them the go-ahead on behalf of the Rootes Group.

The basis of the car was a Mk1 Sceptre floorpan and twin carburettor 1592cc Sceptre engine with the body constructed in the Superleggera fashion of a tubular skeleton with aluminium body panels attached. It featured the Sceptre's twin headlamps and central grille, plus the Sceptre and Alpine's instrumentation. A prototype was produced and enthusiastically received by the local Rootes representatives. It was shipped back to Coventry for assessment before returning to Turin. Touring launched the car, named the Sunbeam Venezia, in St Mark's Square, Venice, on 12 September 1963. Its arrival to the Square was completed on a gondola!

It was proposed that there would be a production run of about 250 cars. It was going to retail at around £1,440, which put it in the same cost bracket as the Super Snipe, Sunbeam Tiger and Mk2 Jaguar. In 1963/4, Rootes finances were in a dire state and that of Touring were not much better. Both companies would be gone by 1967. In the end, only around 200 were made. A number of the cars have survived in the UK and abroad but the Sunbeam Venezia must rank today as one the rarest Rootes cars.

The next major upgrade for the Sceptre came in September 1965 with the release of the Mk2. To freshen the look of the car, it received the front wings and bonnet of the

Above and below: The Sunbeam Venezia, built on a Mk1 Sceptre floorpan.

Mk2 Super Minx. The two Teds (White and Green) in the Design office did a good job while retaining the body of the Mk1 Sceptre. The new look brought in standard size 7-inch (18cm) headlamps with two 5¾-inch (14.6cm) auxiliary lamps set into the full-width grille. A redesigned central main grille was part of the new look. Side lights incorporating the indicators were mounted above the main headlamps under the 'peaks' of the wings. Inside, new seating was fitted using a newly developed breathable plastic material. A new feature was an adjustable steering wheel actioned by turning the steering wheel hub boss to loosen it and then pulling or pushing the steering wheel to suit before relocking. The 'positive' earthing arrangement used for years changed to the now industry standard of a 'negative' earth system.

Under the bonnet the latest 1725cc, five-bearing crankshaft engine was fitted. Added was a crankshaft damper and a new air cleaner assembly. In the age of rationalisation, the engine was also used in the Hillman Super Minx, Minx, Singer Vogue, Gazelle V, Sunbeam Rapier IV and Sunbeam Alpine with different rates of tune and carburation. The Mk2 Sceptre was fitted with a Solex 32 PAIS twin-choke carburettor, giving the engine a power output of 85bhp. The Borg-Warner 35 automatic gearbox was now offered for the first time. Discrete 'Rootes 1725' badging was on the lower part of the front wings of the Rootes car range that used this engine. Duo-tone paint schemes were discontinued on the MK2.

In manual form, the car could reach 60mph in 13.1 second from standstill, some 4 seconds quicker than the Mk1, and could reach a top speed of around 100mph. Compared

NEW HUMBER SCEPTRE *Mark II.*

NEW STYLING – NEW PERFORMANCE – NEW LUXURY

The exciting sports performance is now further improved by a new and powerful 1,725 c.c. engine – with overdrive as standard, or fully-automatic transmission as an extra. Superbly equipped and elegantly styled, the new Humber Sceptre has a roomy interior with luxurious seating, wide and deep all-round vision, front disc brakes, masterly road-holding and ride and many new features. These include smart new frontal styling and interior trim, new driving refinements and travel amenities. This is a prestige car of quality, finely-engineered, reliable and economical – magnificent value.

A ROOTES PRODUCT   NOW WITH POWERFUL NEW '1725' ENGINE

The MK2 Sceptre brochure.

with the contemporary competitors available at the time, which *Autocar* considered to be the Ford Corsair 2000E, Rover 2000SC, Triumph 2000 and Wolseley 18/85, the Mk2 Sceptre pretty much beat the competition in the test categories of maximum speed, 0–60 time, standing start over a quarter of a mile and overall fuel consumption. No estate version was offered. The car retailed at £1,139, which in this group was mid-range. Around 12,000 cars were produced.

As far back as 1963, work had commenced on the next generation that would replace the Hillman Super Minx, Singer Gazelle, Sunbeam Rapier and, of course, Humber. The project title was 'Arrow'.

The story of the Arrow actually traces back to 1960 with what would become the advanced small car, the Hillman Imp, which was the Rootes answer to the BMC Mini. It broke new ground by having a small aluminium engine developed from a Coventry-Climax design and located at the rear and driving the rear wheels. The boot was at the front.

The Imp had a troubled start as Rootes were denied the opportunity to expand Ryton, having to build a new factory in an area of high unemployment as a result of Conservative government policy. Liverpool and Linwood, west of Glasgow, were proposed sites. At Linwood, Pressed Steel had opened a pressing plant and so Rootes opted to head north. It cost some £23 million to construct and set up with the aid of a government loan. Linwood would have to use a workforce predominantly from the declining shipbuilding industry, who were highly unionised and who had had no knowledge of building cars. The car was not fully developed before manufacturing had to start in 1962 for a 1963 launch. The logistics of having the car's mechanical parts produced in Coventry then being transported to Linwood added to the problems and cost, though at least the bodies were manufactured at Pressed Steel, opposite the plant. This would eventually become an integral part of Rootes. The Imp would go on to be produced and was successful once its issues had been resolved.

The nature of the Imp's advance design led to the consideration of a larger version that could replace the Audax range of mid-sized saloons. Bernard Winter had retired as Head of Engineering for Rootes and was replaced by Peter Ware, who brought with him a lot of new ideas and enthusiasm. One of his first development projects, together with stylist Rex Fleming, was the development of 'Project Swallow'. The plan was to have a brand-new floorpan and body, to be fitted with a transversely mounted 6-cylinder all-aluminium engine at the rear with the radiator at the front of the car. A four-door prototype was produced but its design was so complex and reliability of the prototype so poor, with a somewhat ungainly design, that the feasibility of the project was brought into question by the Rootes Board.

It was seen as a project that needed more engineering and financial resource to resolve and as far as the Board was concerned, with the dire financial state that Rootes was in, the project could not be justified and was cancelled. Fortunately, one of the only Swallow prototype cars survived and is kept in the Coventry Transport Museum.

Although Rootes recorded a loss of £200,000 on 31 July 1963, this was an improvement over the £2 million loss in 1962 caused primarily by the strike at British Light Steel Pressings in London, which badly affected production across the range.

It was back to the drawing board and a more tried-and-trusted design was considered the best way forward. Harry Sheron was established as a new lead, reporting to Peter Ware.

Harry built a team around him that included Rex Fleming, whose work on the ill-fated Swallow project was to prove invaluable to the Arrow design team. Peter Ware also brought two new faces into Design, Peter Wilson and Roy Axe. Roy would go on to have an illustrious career by developing the all-new Rapier fastback for 1967 and later moving to Austin-Rover, where he styled many cars before relocating to the United States.

The Arrow would have a motor industry standard MacPherson strut and coil spring suspension at the front and semi-elliptical leaf springs and telescopic dampers at the back. Steering was Burman recirculating ball. There were three engine variants over the years, all four cylinders – 1496cc, 1592cc and the 1725cc. The Sceptre would have the latter. In some quarters it was accepted that Rootes took onboard the plain and simple straightforward engineering of the Mk1 Ford Cortina.

The following comes from notes by Professor Anthony Stevens who was Rootes' Senior Engine Designer. In the autumn of 1963, work commenced on the overall design for the Arrow alongside the Swallow. Initially the car was designed in saloon and estate form for Hillman, Singer and Humber marques. The central section of the ill-fated Swallow prototype car was effectively used, so it was a case of achieving acceptable styling of the front and rear ends. After the Sceptre styling and clay models had been produced and accepted, the saloon was given final design approval in March 1965.

The first pre-prototype Arrow car was completed in August 1964 with other prototypes coming in March 1965. Estate cars were to be saloon conversions with an additional 3 inches (78mm) added length to the floorpan and body behind the rear wheel arches. At this stage, estates would only be offered on the Hillman and Singer cars.

Testing was undertaken during 1964 at the Chobham Military Vehicle Testing Ground in Surrey with prototypes being driven in extremely rough conditions in order to ensure

An early prototype 'Arrow' undergoing testing at Chobham Military Test Site in Surrey. (John Cunningham)

the car would be able to handle all types of road conditions. Trials were also undertaken at Wellesbourne and at MIRA. Once more, I am indebted to Tim Cunningham for sharing his father John's pictures of a prototype Arrow at Chobham. It will be seen that, at this stage, final design for the front and rear had not been agreed.

Once development testing was complete, production tooling was procured and set up in Ryton with Stoke producing the engines, manual transmissions, wheels and axles.

For the Sceptre, its final front and rear styling was signed off in November 1965 with a production date of April 1967. In the same year, the Hawk, Super Snipe and Imperial models stopped being produced. The Sceptre was now the only Humber available.

The Mk3 Arrow Sceptre went on sale in October 1967 adorned with the Chrysler Pentastar, indicating Chrysler's continuing influence as they took further control of the company. Bodies destined to be Sceptres were simply identified on the line and fitted with the enhanced trim. The car came with a comprehensive list of standard equipment including the 1725cc engine with alloy cylinder head, which with the twin Stromberg CD 150 carburettor set-up gave an output of 94bhp; a vinyl roof covering like the Series Imperial; individual front reclining seats; and moulded individual rear seats with a central armrest and cubby hole. There was a walnut-veneer dashboard with eyeball ventilators at each end, walnut wood inserts on the centre console and in the rear compartment. The adjustable-for-reach steering wheel of the Mk2 was retained. There was walnut-veneer trim to all four doors, full instrumentation, and bright anodised aluminium trim to wheel arches, sills and the edge of the boot lid. There was a painted coach line along both sides of the car, a four-headlamp set-up with 5¾-inch dipped and main beam lights, as well as reversing lights, and four-speed manual gearbox with overdrive, with an automatic option. The car had discrete 'Humber' scripts on the front left-hand corner of the bonnet and the right-hand corner of the boot lid. A new Sceptre badge was also created for the rear roof side panel, which was a letter 'S' with the Sceptre mace vertically through it. It went on sale with a retail price of £1,139.

A prototype Mk3 Sceptre in the styling studio, with issues still to resolve.

THE NEW ROOTES SCEPTRE

It is unknown if there was confusion over the make or this was an inter-market picture – seen here is an early publicity image of the 'Rootes' Sceptre.

Above and left: The plush interior of the Mk3 Sceptre.

With the Mk3 Sceptre launched, all the previous Audax-based range of cars stopped.

The Arrow Sceptre was exported to Europe and around the world and would also be assembled from CKD kits in those countries with assembly plants. A lucrative deal was arranged by Rootes to send CKD kits of the Hunter to Iran. A brand-new factory was built to assemble the cars, known in Iran as the 'Paykan', which was Persian for 'Arrow'. They just built basic saloons using the parts sent from Ryton and gradually began making their own parts and own models, but the Sceptre was never sent out. This deal generated millions of pounds for Chrysler UK until the project ended in 2005.

Some markets had different tariffs or issues that affected the make of the car brought to that country. As an example, the German market recognised Sunbeam more than Humber so the 'Sunbeam Sceptre' was sold into these territories with corresponding UK-based publicity brochures using doctored images with 'Humber' badging removed.

The German brochure for the Sunbeam Sceptre.

Wenn je ein Wagen Lob verdiente, dann ist's der neue Sunbeam Sceptre. Nicht nur für seine gediegene Linie. Oder für die Qualität und die Vollständigkeit seiner Ausstattung. Oder für sein ruhiges, angenehmes Fahren. Vor allem verdient er Lob für die Vereinigung dieser Eigenschaften mit Sparsamkeit im Betrieb und mit einer Leistung, die vielen 2-Liter-Limousinen überlegen ist. Der fabelhaft ausgestattete neue Sunbeam Sceptre bietet viel, sehr viel fürs Geld.

Der beachtenswerte neue

SUNBEAM SCEPTRE

4 Türen, 1,7 Liter-Motor, elektrischer Schnellgang

EN VERKOERPERT DEN WILLEN DER ROOTES, RESOLUT VORANZUGEHEN

A boost to Rootes came in 1968 in a competition that they had not really shown interest in – the London to Sydney Marathon. This inaugural event, sponsored by the *Daily Express* and the *Sydney Daily Telegraph,* was to cover 10, 373 miles driving through Europe and Asia before crossing to Australia and finishing in Sydney. Three drivers, Andrew Cowan, Colin Malkin and Brian Coyle, took a modified 'Arrow' Hillman Hunter and out of ninety-four starters they went on to win the event. This caught out Rootes, who had never envisaged this. To maximise the publicity that emanated from this event, Rootes produced a new range of brochures to capitalise on the win and to demonstrate the durability of the Arrow-based cars.

A new car had been in development since 1967 after the completion of the Arrow project – the Avenger. This all-new car was the 'B' car designed alongside the ill-fated 'C' car, which, as has been seen in the Series car chapter, would have been a new generation Humber. The Avenger was to be built in the Ryton plant, which would put pressure on the existing production lines, so a decision was taken in 1969 to switch Arrow car production to Linwood alongside the Imp.

One of the development cars assembled in France came to the Design Department in Humber Road, Stoke, to be fitted with a 1725cc engine and have a new design of 'Sceptre' script added to its rear flanks. The project did not progress and the car design became the '180' in the UK and Europe.

Once production started at Linwood, the chassis number sequence changed to identify cars produced there. Early cars produced in Ryton from 1967 to 1969 had a chassis number sequence commencing 'B111xxxxxx'. For Linwood, the 'B' was replaced and became 'LH/G/H' series, 'L' denoting Linwood.

The first of the upgrades following this upheaval came in 1972 with a revised ratios manual gearbox and new wheel trims. The adjustable-reach steering wheel fell foul of new European safety legislation for crash performance.

Major changes to the parent company happened on 30 June 1970 when 'Rootes Motors Ltd' became 'Chrysler UK Ltd'. As a consequence of Chrysler taking full control of the business, the Linwood factories (the ex-Pressed Steel plant and the car assembly plant) became 'Chrysler Scotland Ltd'.

William Rootes's son Geoffrey, who had become the second Lord Rootes on his father's death, relinquished his role as Chairman of Chrysler UK in June 1973 and retired. Gilbert Hunt, from Massey Ferguson, took over as Chairman.

1974 saw the next major upgrade to the Mk3 Sceptre with new trim to the seats using a lined velour material and Triplex Sundym green-tinted glass fitted to all windows.

An estate was added, which was the basic body available from 1967 on the Hillman Minx and Singer Vogue. Being a Sceptre, it had a range of additional luxury items added including a built-in aluminium roof rack with a faux-wood insert along the side rails and two slideable cross-bars. There was wood effect on the 'D' post surrounding the chromed vent grilles. A wood-effect panel was added to the tailgate together with reversing lights and a wash-wiper. On the saloon, a new anodised aluminium panel was placed across the back, below the boot lid, encompassing a flap for the fuel filler cap. Revised-design hubcaps were also fitted. Both saloon and estate had redesigned bumpers. The automatic gearbox was now four speeds – the Borg-Warner 45.

With Chrysler now fully in charge, other new generation models were coming through such as the Roy Axe-designed Chrysler Alpine, Horizon and Chrysler Sunbeams.

86

The 1974 final version of the MK3 Sceptre.

The Sceptre estate.

On 16 July 1976 the last Sceptre rolled off the Linwood production line, bringing to an end Humber as a marque.

Two years later the troubled Chrysler UK Ltd was taken over by Peugeot SA and became Peugeot-Talbot Ltd. They invested heavily in the Ryton plant, which would go on to produce the UK-based Peugeot 309 model, the 405 four-door saloon and estate, and the small 206 and SW (station wagon) versions. Ryton finally closed on 31 December 2006.

The Whitley design centre was sold to Jaguar Land Rover. Both Stoke and Ryton sites were demolished, with housing being built at Stoke and industrial units at Ryton. Roads in these areas were named in honour of Rootes car models.

Peugeot-Talbot still retained the rights to the old Rootes model names and oddly brought out special editions of existing cars in the 1980s and 1990s. In 1983 a special edition Talbot Solara was called the Sceptre and a Talbot Horizon special edition was called the Pullman. Both cars had a duo-tone colour scheme, special extras and improved trim. As late as 1991, there were special edition models of the '205', '405' and '605' Peugeots called 'Sceptre' with appropriate badging.

6

Chassis Numbers (As Known)

Model	Year	Commencing	Final
Humber Hawk Mk I Chassis only	1945	2700001	
Humber Hawk Mk I	1945–1947	2710001	2710984
	1945–1947	2720001	2720239
Humber Hawk Mk I Export RHD	1945–1947	2730001	2730043
Humber Hawk Mk I Export LHD	1945–1947	2740001	2740451
Humber Hawk Mk II	1947–1948	5800001	5804000
Humber Hawk Mk III	1948–1950	5900001	5908054
Humber Hawk Mk III CKD	1948–1950	5920001	5921986
Humber Hawk Mk IV	1950–1952	A5000001	A5079828
Humber Hawk Mk IV CKD	1950–1952	A5030001	A5032664
Humber Hawk Mk V	1952–1954	A5200001	A5212710
Humber Hawk Mk V CKD	1952–1954	A5220001	A5221590
Humber Hawk Mk VI	1954–1955	A5400001	A5413947
	1954–1955	A5420001	A5426061
Humber Hawk Mk VIA Deluxe	1956–1957	A5460001	A5463535
Humber Hawk Mk VI CKD	1956–1957	A5450001	A5451962
	1956–1957	A5453001	A5454878
Humber Super Snipe	1939	8100500	81011477
	1939–1940	8200500	8200695
Humber Super Snipe Mk l Chassis	1945–1948	8700001	8700344
Humber Super Snipe Mk l UK	1945–1948	8710001	8711153
Humber Super Snipe Mk l	1945–1948	8720001	?
Humber Super Snipe Mk l RHD Export	1945–1948	8730001	8730878
Humber Super Snipe Mk l LHD Export	1945–1948	8740001	8740772
Humber Super Snipe Mk l CKD	1945–1948	8770001	8770762
Humber Super Snipe Mk ll	1948–1950	8800001	8807287
Humber Super Snipe Mk ll CKD	1948–1950	8810001	8811074
Humber Super Snipe Mk lll	1950–1952	A8000001	A8007679
Humber Super Snipe Mk lll CKD	1950–1952	A8010001	A8010324
Humber Super Snipe Mk lll Heavy Duty	1950–1952	A8020001	A8020700

Model	Year	Commencing	Final
Humber Super Snipe Mk lV	1952–1954	A8200001	A8205988
Humber Super Snipe Mk lV CKD	1952–1954	A8215001	A8217508
Humber Super Snipe Mk lV Heavy Duty	1952–1954	A8250001	A8251353
Humber Super Snipe Mk lVA	1954–1955	A8400001	A8400651
Humber Super Snipe MK lVB	1955–1958	A8410001	A8411272
Humber Super Snipe Mk lVA CKD	1954–1955	A8430001	A8430324
Humber Super Snipe Mk lVA Heavy Duty	1954–1955	A8450001	A8450025
Humber Super Snipe MK lVB Heavy Duty	1955–1958	A8450101	A8450460
Humber Super Snipe MK lVB CKD	1955–1958	A8460001	A8460720
Humber Hawk Series l	1957–1959	A5700001	A5709321
Humber Hawk Series lA	1959–1960	B5000001	B5006347
Humber Hawk Series ll	1960–1962	B5100001	B5106974
Humber Hawk Series lll	1962–1964	B5200001	B5206241
Humber Hawk Series lV	1964–1966	B54000001	B54002031
Humber Hawk Series lVA	1966–1967	B054600001	B054603787
Humber Super Snipe Series l (Pre-production)	1958–1959	A8500001	A8500004
Humber Super Snipe Series l	1958–1959	A8900001	A8905512
Humber Super Snipe Series l CKD	1958–1959	A8975001	A8975956
Humber Super Snipe Series ll	1959–1960	B8000001	B8005597
Humber Super Snipe Series ll CKD	1959–1960	B8080001	B8183084
Humber Super Snipe Series lll	1960–1962	B8100001	B8107257
Humber Super Snipe Series lll CKD	1960–1962	B8180001	B8183084
Humber Super Snipe Series lV	1962–1964	B8200001	B8206495
Humber Super Snipe Series lV CKD	1962–1964	B8280001	B828 ?
Humber Super Snipe Series V	1964–1965	B84000001	B840 ?
Humber Super Snipe Series V CKD	1964–1965	B84800001	B84800108 ?
Humber Super Snipe Series VA	1965–1967	B084600001	B084601731
Humber Super Snipe Series VA CKD	1965–1967	B084700001	B084701338 ?
Humber Imperial Series V	1964–1965	B84300001	B84301189
Humber Imperial Series VA	1965–1967	B884400001	B884401119
Humber Sceptre MK l (Twin Carb)	1963–1964	B3100001	B3115312
Humber Sceptre MK l CKD (Twin Carb)	1963–1964	B3150001	B315 ?
Humber Sceptre MK IA (Single Carb)	Feb 64	B3111403	B311 ?
Humber Sceptre MK IB (Single Carb)	1964–1965	B31200001	B31207392
Humber Sceptre MK IB CKD (Single Carb)	1964–1965	B31250001	B312?
Humber Sceptre MK ll	1965–1967	B132000001	B132011985
Humber Sceptre MK lll	1967–1968	B111000001	B111006790
Humber Sceptre MK lll CKD	1967–1968	B111900001	B1119?

Model	Year	Commencing	Final
Humber Sceptre MK lll	1969	B112000001	B1120501851
	1969–1970	LB112500001	LB ?
	1970–1971	LG112 600001	LG112 631873
	1971–1972	LH090 600001	LH112 721181
	1972–1973	L3090 600001	L3090 802708
	1973–1974	L4090 100001	L4090 121044
	1974–1975	L5*** ******	L5 ?
	1975–1976	L6*** ******	L6 ?
	1974–1976	RSABE5L100000	RSABE5L ?
	1974–1976	RSABE6L100000	RSABE6L ?
	1974–1976	RSABM5L100000	RSABM5L ?
	1974–1976	RSABM6L100000	RSABM6L ?

Clubs and Support

The Post Vintage Humber Car Club was formed in 1974 to cater for the interests of owners of Humber cars made after 1931, when the Rootes Brothers took control of Humber and began to impress their own identity on new car designs.

We publish a bi-monthly magazine called *Old Faithful*, in recognition of Lord Field Marshal Bernard Montgomery's open-tourer Humber Snipe staff car.

We hold an extensive collection of Humber technical literature, brochures and archive material, with the bulk of this book being compiled from this source.

There are regional meeting groups, an annual rally and local events. The Club has registrars for Mark, Series and Sceptre models and there is help available for answering technical queries and where to locate spares.

A past rally held at Woburn Abbey estate, when just over 200 cars were present.

The Club has embarked on a major programme of remanufacturing parts, at present for the Series cars, including wheel arch repair sections, sill sections and chassis parts, as well as chrome parts including door handles and rear light plinths. It can also help with tracing parts.

In the UK, we deal with issues associated with retaining original registrations for cars that have lost registration documentation or have out-of-date registration documents, liaising as appropriate with DVLA on behalf of members.

The Club is a member of the Association of Rootes Car Clubs and actively assists and supports the valuable work of the Rootes Archive Centre Trust (www.rootesarchive.org) to provide access to original Rootes Group technical drawings and data on behalf of all Rootes clubs in the UK and overseas.

The Club can be contacted through its website, www.humber.org.uk, and has a large presence on Facebook. The website carries a lot of detailed information on the cars with road tests and brochures.

Many Humber and Rootes clubs exist around the world, especially in original export markets, and these can be easily found through internet search engines.

Spare Parts

The youngest Humbers are over forty years old now, but between the Clubs and the following list of contacts, which is not exhaustive, there is support to keep these cars in running order. Unfortunately, rust tends to be one issue that can get cars taken off the road, hence why the investment in the remanufacturing of key panels has been a priority for the Club and specialists. Mechanical and electrical components can also be rebuilt or purchased for the benefit of Humber owners.

The following are able to help with support in providing services for our Humbers.

Norfolk Humbers – predominately remanufactures structural parts for Series cars. Water pumps, brake callipers, brake servos, power-steering parts and second-hand parts as appropriate. They can also source parts for Mark and Sceptre cars, and offer a postage service.
Contact: Glen Bunting
Tel: 07799 216533
Email: glen@norfolkhumbers.co.uk
www.norfolkhumbers.co.uk

Speedy Spares – Established in 1965, a Rootes Group specialist that offer parts for Series, Mark and Sceptres. They have a shop in East Sussex, UK, and offer a postage service.
Tel: 01273 417889 or 412764
www.speedyspares.co.uk

Arrows – Based near Southampton, Paul Marshall offers a restoration and parts service for Rootes cars – predominantly Arrow-based cars including Sceptres.
Tel: 01489 877580
www.arrow5.co.uk

Steve Osbourne – Small-scale remanufacturing of critical rubber parts and refinishing of key components. Predominantly focused on Series cars.
Tel: 07971 526542
Email: Stephenaozz@gmail.com

Rootes Parts – Based in the Netherlands. Can supply parts, either new old stock or remanufactured, for numerous Rootes vehicles.
www.rootesparts.com

Acknowledgements

I must first record my grateful thanks to my wife, Andrea, for putting up with my 'hobby' for all these years and proofreading. Thanks also to my daughter Hannah for proofreading and helping with text and picture issues. David Clark, Richard Gruet and Aubrey Pinchbeck for helping with proofreading and assisting me with the text, pictures and invaluable technical information. Also the Post Vintage Humber Car Club committee for their support; Graham Robson and Richard Langworth for their knowledge and assistance; James Spencer and Andy Bye of the Rootes Archive Centre Trust, who helped with sourcing illustrations; and Geoff Carverhill, author of *The Rootes Story* and *The Commer Story* for all his help and support. Finally to Amberley Publishing for suggesting this book.

All illustrations in this book are from the archive of the Post Vintage Humber Car Club except where acknowledged. Every attempt has been made to seek permission for copyright material used in this book. However, if we have inadvertently used copyright material without permission or acknowledgement, we apologise and will make the necessary correction at the first opportunity.

The author and publisher would like to thank the following people/organisations for permission to use copyright material in this book:

James Spencer and Andy Bye of the Rootes Archive Centre Trust
David Clark
Tim Cunningham
Richard Langworth
Richard Gruet
Denis and Darren Cunningham
Keith Bagnall
Keith Anderson
Ray Sellers

Bibliography

Bradley, Robert Penn, *Armstrong Siddeley The Postwar Cars* (MRP Publications, 1989)
Carverhill, Geoff, *The Rootes Story* (The Crowood Press, 2019)
Freeman, Tony, *Humber – An Illustrated History 1868–1976* (Academy Books, 1991. Reprinted 2011)
Langworth, Richard, *Tiger, Alpine, Rapier* (Osprey Publishing Ltd, 1982)
Robson, Graham, *Cars of the Rootes Group* (MRP Publications, 1990)
Rowe, David, *Rootes Cars of the 1950s, 1960s & 1970s: A Pictorial History* (Veloce, 2015)
Young, Daniel, *Humber Anthology 1946–1976* (1991)